LET THE WATERS
ROAR

LET THE WATERS ROAR

EVANGELISTS IN THE GULAG

Georgi Vins
compiler

BAKER BOOK HOUSE

Grand Rapids, Michigan 49516

ISBN: 0-8010-9308-2

Second printing, March 1990

Printed in the United States of America

Scripture quotations are from the King James Version of the Bible.

Contents

Foreword

Because the testimonies in this book were originally shared with Christians in the Soviet Union, the audiences were familiar both with the persecuted church and with the Soviet penal system. Western readers, however, may wonder about certain passages. Therefore, some preliminary explanations will help the reader to better understand and appreciate the experiences of these Russian believers.

First of all, the Soviet penal system has many levels. A Soviet citizen suspected of violating the Criminal Code can be arrested and locked in a prison's "investigation cell" without a trial. The citizen remains in that cell while a government prosecutor conducts an investigation and builds his case against the prisoner. At the trial, the prisoner may be sentenced to a term in prison, a term in a labor camp, a term of exile in an isolated village, a term of servitude on a government forced-labor project, or to some combination of the above. Sane prisoners (including Christians) have also been sentenced to indefinite periods in special psychiatric hospitals. Thus,

Russian Christians use the general term *in bonds* not necessarily to mean "in shackles" but to indicate one's presence in one of these locations.

Sometimes these testimonies are intentionally vague on certain points. For example, a former prisoner may refer to getting a secret message out of a labor camp without the censor's knowledge but not reveal how he did it. It should be obvious, however, that publishing how such a feat was accomplished would be foolish. Such information could jeopardize the safety of a courier or give Soviet authorities clues on how to prevent future messages.

Likewise, believers do not always explain exactly which Christian activities caused their arrest or who else was helping them. Again, even after a prisoner has been freed, he may need to keep silent on certain subjects. If Soviet authorities were to gain new revelations on a former prisoner's Christian activities, fresh charges could be raised against him or against others. On at least one occasion, Soviet authorities have used an article from the West as evidence against Christians arrested for secretly printing Bibles.

Persecuted Christians also tend to gloss over details of their own sufferings even when no security is at stake. The reason is understandable: Christians who love God enough to endure great hardships for him are not interested in portraying their own courage or hardiness. Rather, they are living to glorify their Lord, so they emphasize the mercy, comfort, and blessings he provided despite the harsh conditions.

Finally, while recounting their experiences, the individuals in this book sometimes refer to other Christians who live in their home towns or whom they met in the gulag. Occasionally they also mention Christians of the past who were martyred at the hands of the authorities. Readers who wish to learn more about these believers and their sufferings will want to consult the biographical supplement at the end of the book.

Introduction

When my family lived in Kiev, we were given a large, beautiful painting. On it was portrayed a raging sea, tempestuous clouds, and large waves pounding against enormous stones and cliffs. The picture was in a handsome frame. But the most important thing about the painting was the words written on the dark background of the sky and waves, excerpts from the first three verses of Psalm 46:

> God is our refuge and strength. . . . Therefore we will not fear . . . though the waters roar!

We hung the painting on our living room wall, and its message encouraged our whole family during difficult days and trials for many years. More than ten times during those years the authorities conducted searches and confiscated Bibles, Gospels, cassettes, and Christian hymns and sermons. Even personal letters with references to the name of God were taken.

But the painting continued to hang on the wall, and those words—*God is our refuge and strength. . . . There-*

fore we will not fear . . . though the waters roar!—were read by the people who conducted searches in our house. They were also read by the Christians who came to visit us.

In March 1974 I was arrested, and in January 1975 I was brought to trial in Kiev. The public prosecutor charged me with nine accusations, all of them on a religious theme, including preaching the gospel and printing Bibles. The court sentenced me to five years' deprivation of freedom in strict-regime labor camps plus five years of exile. On top of that, they handed down a third penalty: the confiscation of all personal property! This third punishment was intended to hurt my family.

Soon after the trial, I was transported to one of the labor camps near the city of Yakutsk in Siberia. Some time later, during a visit to the camp, my family told me how the confiscation of property had proceeded.

When the sentence went into effect, a special commission had arrived at our house to take inventory for confiscation: the table, the chairs, the buffet, a book shelf, the couch, the washing machine, the refrigerator, dishes, and so on. The commission even decided to confiscate the painting on which was written *God is our refuge and strength. . . . Therefore we will not fear . . . though the waters roar!*

During the confiscation, another Christian, Ivan Petrovich, happened to drop by our house. He sat on the couch, which had already been entered into the record, and silently observed what was happening. One of the commission members took the painting down from the wall and stood it alongside the furniture earmarked for removal.

Another commission member, a young woman, was

writing a description of each object in the pile. But when she got to the painting, she was puzzled: How should it be recorded? "What's the name of this painting?" she asked aloud. "How should I enter it?"

No one answered. The other members of the commission were walking through the house, checking outside, and looking in the shed for other things to confiscate. In the room where the young woman was writing up her inventory were only my wife, children, and Ivan Petrovich.

The woman lifted the painting, set it on the table, and asked again, "What should I call this? How should I enter it in the record?"

Ivan Petrovich stood up, stepped over to the table, took the painting in his hands, and said, "Write just what's written here: 'God is our refuge and strength. . . . Therefore we will not fear . . . though the waters roar!'"

The young woman was pleased to find a name for the painting and started to write it hurriedly onto her document. She wrote: "A painting with the words, 'god is our refuge and strength. . . .'"

"Why the word *God* with a small *g*?" Ivan Petrovich objected. "On the painting it has a capital letter. Write it the way it's written on the painting!"

The woman corrected the letter and wrote the word *God* with a capital letter. But she soon stopped writing and was obviously not going to enter the whole name of the painting, so Ivan Petrovich prompted her: "Please be good enough to write the full name of the painting for the record. Do you want me to dictate it to you?" So he dictated to her the whole text on the picture. "'God is our refuge and strength. . . . Therefore we will not fear . . . though the waters roar!'"

The young lady started to write down the name in full, but then she asked aloud, "What are we taking this picture for? Who needs it? Only believers!"

At that point the other members of the commission entered the room. One of them, glancing at the document, asked, "What's all this stuff about God that you've written into the record? 'God is our refuge and strength'?"

"That's the long name of the painting that you took from the wall for confiscation," she answered.

As it turned out, this man was the head of the commission. He was obviously irritated with such an entry and said, "You've spoiled the whole record with this painting! And who's going to buy it from us with such a name?"

Then he said to my wife, "By law, you have the right to make the first purchase of items confiscated here by the government. This is your lawful right!"

But my wife remained silent.

Then he turned to Ivan Petrovich. "As I understand it, you're also a believer?"

"Yes, I also believe in God, who is our refuge and strength!"

"Maybe you'll buy this painting from the government?" the official asked. Then he pointed at the document and the furniture and said, "All these confiscated objects already belong to the government. We can sell the furniture and painting to anyone we want. Buy this painting from us! What are we going to do with it? We don't need this painting. We won't ask much for it. Just five rubles!"

Ivan Petrovich pulled five rubles out of his pocket and presented it to the commission. Next, taking the painting, he triumphantly hung it on the wall in its original spot and loudly read, "'God is our refuge and strength. . . . Therefore we will not fear . . . though the waters roar!'"

And so this painting remained in our house, proclaiming the strength and might of God, and encouraging and comforting the hearts of the many believers persecuted for faith in Christ who visited our home in Kiev.

But persecution for trusting in the Lord is not new in my homeland. It has now been a little over one hundred years since evangelical Christianity began in Russia. In 1867 Nikita Voronin became the first Russian baptized in faith. Right from his first days of following the Lord, Voronin endured great persecution for his faith in Christ. Almost the entire history of the Evangelical Christian-Baptist believers in my country has been characterized by persecution, suffering for the truth of Christ in prisons, exile, labor camps, and even psychiatric hospitals. But what can separate us from the love of God? Can grief, persecution, famine, or sword? No, there is no one and nothing that can separate us from the love of God in Christ Jesus. ". . . in all these things we are more than conquerors through him that loved us" (Rom. 8:37).

Now the Lord has helped the staff of International Representation to collect and translate into English the precious testimonies of present-day Russian believers, testimonies of suffering and blessing. These are the stories of those who walk the narrow, thorny path in the footprints of Christ. We place this material into your hands, brothers and sisters in Christ who live in the West. Through it, may the Lord bless your hearts to love Jesus Christ more, to cherish your Bible, and to pray for spiritual revival throughout the world, and especially in your own land.

Please do not forget to pray for the work of the gospel

in Russia, and for those who even today are enduring trials and hardships for their faith in Christ.

> Georgi P. Vins
> International Representation
> for the Evangelical Baptist Churches
> of the Soviet Union

Georgi Vins

Georgi Vins (b. 1928) spent eight years in Soviet prisons and labor camps for preaching the gospel and serving as general secretary of the Council of Evangelical Baptist Churches (CEBC). In April 1979, halfway through a ten-year sentence, the 50-year-old Vins was suddenly stripped of his Soviet citizenship and exiled to the United States as part of a prisoner exchange between the two countries. The CEBC then appointed Vins to be its representative abroad and to inform the West of the repression and persecution of Soviet Christians, a ministry he continues today from headquarters in Elkhart, Indiana. Vins and his wife, Nadia, have five children.

Baptism, communion, prayer, family devotions and witnessing are integral to church vitality and growth in the Soviet Union and around the world.

1

Andrei Yudintsev
A Teen in the Gulag

The guards took me to the investigation cell and opened the door. For the first time, I saw prison bunks and inmates. Their faces looked strange, with a searching, penetrating stare.

I stepped forward, and the prisoners immediately started asking me questions: Where was I from? What was I in for? Most of all they were interested in my character, what I was like as a person. I silently prayed that the Lord himself would guide my lips, and I started to tell my story.

In the beginning, I had not even thought that I would

Andrei Yudintsev (b. 1964) was just 18 when police arrested him at a Christian youth meeting in 1982. He spent the next three and a half years in Soviet prisons and labor camps. Barely four weeks before Andrei was released, his father, Vasily, was arrested for his Christian ministry and later sentenced to seven years in bonds. The oldest of thirteen children, Andrei now serves in the Soviet army, a duty mandatory for all young men. Soviet military life is not easy for anyone; but cruel harrassment makes it even more difficult for Christians.

19

end up in bonds. When the police took some of us from the Thanksgiving worship service to the police station, I thought they would keep us for fifteen days or fine us. At that time the desires of my flesh and spirit were opposite. The flesh wanted freedom. At the age of eighteen—which is still quite young—I was not really willing to be imprisoned in a hard, unfamiliar place. Although I knew from stories what it was like, somehow I didn't want to go myself. But in the end, they put me behind bars.

On the following day, conversation in our cell resumed. We discussed—even debated—many different subjects, each one giving his own point of view. I always tried to answer with passages from the Bible. My mother taught me that. When people ask you questions, try to answer from the Word of God; only then will the answer be complete. I remembered this and with the Lord's help tried to answer that way. Life passed this way for about a month—continual discussions, constant questioning—until one day I was handcuffed and taken to the people's court in Khartsyzsk. My friend Vladimir Timchuk was already there, also handcuffed.

Near the court building we saw many of our friends, but they were not allowed inside. When we were led into the courtroom, I saw that it was full, with representatives from factories, schools, colleges, executive committees. There simply wasn't room left for our Christian friends.

When the trial started, I saw Mama trying to get into the courtroom, but the guards would not permit her inside.

"What is this? Even Mother isn't allowed," I said to the judge.

So they let go of her, and she and several friends were

allowed to enter. The examination began. They read the accusations.

"Do you plead guilty?"

"No, we don't," was our answer.

Then they began to interrogate the witnesses. I had never even seen them before. I asked them questions: "Where was I arrested?" They all gave different answers—that I was on the street behind a fence, or near the doors, near the exit from the building. Of course, these testimonies were incorrect. I asked the judge, "How can they testify when they weren't even there at the moment in question?"

Of course, the judge tried to help the witnesses, and his questions led them out of such confusing situations. But all the same it was clear to the whole auditorium that this was a setup.

Vladimir and I already understood that it was the court's duty to convict and sentence us. And the officials achieved their goals. But somehow Vladimir and I didn't worry; we committed everything to the Lord. We accepted the sentence as from his hand.

After the trial Vladimir and I were put together because of repairs in other cells. God so miraculously closed the eyes of the guards that they failed to realize we were together. When the guards led me to that cell and I saw Vladimir, I could hardly believe he was there. At first Vladimir did not even recognize me because he was occupied with his own business. He was sitting on the second bunk; everyone was looking at him, and he was explaining something. I walked right up to him, set down my belongings and the flimsy mattress given to me, and started listening to him. He turned toward me and could hardly believe his eyes. We embraced and immediately prayed together, praising the Lord. Then we cheered up and started to sing.

When Vladimir was called for transport, we prayed together and said warm farewells. Several days later the guards summoned me for transport, too, and on April 18 I arrived at the camp.

Camp, of course, is very different from prison. Everything is in the open air. I worked the whole year as a welder. It was hard: half of the shift you carry stock, the other half you weld steel. I worked three shifts—the first, second, and the third every week. I particularly remember the second shift, especially in the summer. At dusk I climbed to the roof of the shop, followed the sun beyond the horizon with my eyes, and sang, "The sun vanished behind the horizon; twilight descended over the earth." There's much comfort in that song. I would pray and then climb down to work again. I watched the sun so often.

Of course, that first year was an ordeal. I didn't know how to live among criminals. But the men whom I had met back in prison in my home town graciously watched out for me. Since they had arrived at the camp earlier, they already knew how to get along and gave me hints on how to behave in those circumstances.

"How are you going to live in the camp?" someone asked.

"The same way I lived in freedom—as a Christian," I said. "I want to live the same way and not back off from my beliefs even here. That's my desire."

They understood me and even respected me for this. It was hard, because I was the only Christian in camp. But there were always letters from friends when it was especially hard and lonely. Since the Lord prompted friends to write at those times, letters arrived that were exactly what my spirit needed. This was very comforting, and I greatly rejoiced in such perfect timing. That simply amazed me, and I didn't know how to thank the Lord. In this way he revealed that he is the Lord and that he is faithful to his promises, even though we are sometimes unfaithful. Whenever I was in a dejected condition, God immediately saw my need.

I had been in the camp about two years when one day a friend in another barracks said to me, "They've brought another Christian here."

"Who is he and where is he?" I asked.

"There he is, right in this room, two aisles over."

The face was unfamiliar. He was talking, and other prisoners were questioning him. Then someone called him and he walked over to me with a smile. Evidently they had told him that there was another believer and pointed to me. Without even asking who I was, he walked up and greeted me.

"Where are you from? Do you know . . . ?" I started asking him, naming several Christian families.

"Yes, I know them all," he said.

"Do you know the Yudintsevs?"

"Yes, I know the mother," he said.

I told him that I was her son, and immediately thought, *Praise God, that he has sent me a friend in these conditions.* The newcomer, too, rejoiced, and we went out to thank the Lord. My life with Pavel Zinchenko had begun.

Pavel and I struggled together: we carried all our troubles and shared our failures. When things were hard for me, I ran to him. We talked together and prayed. He came to me with his troubles and family matters. We shared everything to carry it to the Lord and found great comfort in our friendship. Every day we were amazed that we could fellowship together, and we maintained these relations discreetly, so the authorities would not notice and forbid us from meeting.

Pavel and I lived this way for almost a year. Then they brought another Christian to our camp, Vladimir Vlasenko from Nikolaev. He was a good fellow—very stable and cheerful—who had suffered more than either of us. They transferred him from another camp because he had repeatedly asked the authorities for a Bible. When they refused, he took a stand for the right to have the Word of God. As a punishment they transferred him to a different camp.

We gave Vladimir our New Testament right away. His was the very highest bunk, just under the ceiling. There was no air up there at night, but he was happy, because he could turn toward the wall and read the New Testament by the night light. The Lord blessed him, and he never became depressed. The authorities persecuted him; they constantly wore him down. They dug down into every little trifle, but he always told us about his troubles with a smile. The fact that he was standing strongly without getting depressed encouraged us, too. We thanked the Lord for him.

Vladimir, Pavel, and I received many letters from friends all over around holidays. Each received up to thirty letters a day. We read the letters to each other and felt as if we were in fellowship with many thousands of people. The Lord saw our need and provided bits of news, best wishes, and exhortations from our friends.

Shortly before New Year's Day of 1985, God provided a quiet room for us. We prayed fervently, with tears, then embraced and wished each other a happy new year. It was a very glad time.

Soon, however, we all noticed that difficult ordeals began for us. Pavel, the camp artist, was driven out of his job. The leader of the operative division got him sent to hard labor. But Pavel didn't get depressed. Being a welder, he settled down there, did the work, and welded good seams.

Vladimir kept getting punished. Once they even lied about him, saying that he had not spent the night in his barracks, that he had been in another barracks. But that night he had not even gone outside; he slept on his bunk the whole time. The monitor even confirmed that he had not seen anyone leave. Neither had the orderly, but the officer from the operative division stood by his words, that he had a report from a convict that Vlasenko had not spent the night in the barracks.

At the end of January the authorities confiscated the New Testament. I used to carry it in my side pocket in order to read it quickly in my spare time. One day at work some officers came and started to search the shop. When they got to my area, they ordered me to stand up. They searched me and found the New Testament. As soon as I got back to the barracks that evening, I was summoned to the operative division, where orders had been given to lock me in an isolation cell.

"This book isn't forbidden," I said. "You don't have any law anywhere for locking people in isolation for Christian literature. This isn't a forbidden book, and I have the right to own five books in camp."

"I don't know anything," the officer said. "The supervisor authorized seven days for you. If you have any grievances, talk to him. I'm just doing my duty."

At that time Pavel was already locked up there, also for seven days. He had one day left. Knowing that he was there, I asked to be put in the same cell. Of course, our meeting in the cell was very joyous. We talked a long time.

Toward evening they let Pavel out. But when I was down to my last day, waiting out my final hours, I heard them bringing him in again. I knew it was Pavel from his voice. I ran over to the grating and cried, "Pavel, is that you?"

"Yes, yes," he said. "Andrei, they're moving Vladimir and me out of the camp."

What a hard blow! We immediately wished blessings to each other, calling through the grating. Pavel and Vladimir were supposed to be transferred to other camps in the morning.

I didn't sleep all night. In the morning, when I was let out of the isolation cell around eight o'clock, I saw Vladimir and Pavel through a crack in a fence. I called to Pavel. He quickly ran over, with a guard right behind him. The guard pulled him by the collar, but Pavel grabbed the fence between us with one hand while he thrust the other hand through the hole. We grasped hands. Vladimir ran over, too, also with tears, and we said good-bye to each other.

It was very painful to part under those circumstances. When my friends were taken from the camp, everyone watched me. All eyes and ears were on me. Everyone wanted to see how I, who had been so bold when the three of us were together, would act now that I was alone again.

But the Lord strengthened me. The New Testament was given back. People had torn out some pages for themselves. I never learned who had the beginning, or who had the end, but the middle of the New Testament

After his release, Andrei joins his mother, grandmother, and little brothers and sisters on their knees as they offer a prayer of thanksgiving to God for preserving him and keeping him faithful during his confinement in prison.

was left to me to the end of my term. The Lord miraculously preserved it. Twice the authorities wanted to take the New Testament away and it was already in their hands. But I prayed, and the Lord marvelously returned it to me, proof of his all-powerful hand. All during this time, what grieved me very much was that I was sometimes at the end of myself, but the Lord proved to be faithful to his promises and to his Word.

When I had just half a year left until the end of my sentence, I worked as a carpenter. There was a lot of work. We repaired offices, and I decided the time would pass faster if I just got absorbed in work. I was right: time passed so quickly that I scarcely noticed.

Several days before my release, Mama and the young

children came for a short visit. Mama was crying as she told me that Father was arrested. For several years he had been serving the Lord in hiding.

I had often dreamed about meeting with Father after my release. I even planned what we would talk about. I wanted to see him very much. During that last visit with Mama, whatever we talked about, whatever questions we discussed, we always returned to the subject of his arrest.

The last days before my release were sad because of my father's arrest. Before, when I had not known, my heart secretly rejoiced that soon I would be free and would see everyone, but now it was hard to bear this news. I found out that he was charged with anti-Sovietism, speaking against the government authorities. I know that my father, as a Christian, would never do such a thing.

Finally I was released after three and a half years of imprisonment. At first it might seem that this was a waste of my youth, but when it was over, nothing remained except gratitude to the Lord and gladness. David says in Psalm 33, "For our heart shall rejoice in him, because we have trusted in his holy name" (v. 21).

It will always turn out that way, and it came true in my own life. Every circumstance and every hardship amounted to this: that the Lord displayed his merciful right hand, and he marvelously blessed.

Praise only him for everything.

2

Valentina Saveleva
Surviving the Valley of Death

I was arrested while transporting Christian literature. Before my trial, I was imprisoned in Stavropol for almost six months. When in prison for the first time, there is a lot you don't understand. You don't immediately recognize everything that is going on, but the authorities watch you. They study you carefully and use deceptive tricks to glean information from you. One method is to persuade other prisoners to collaborate and draw you into conversation. Since their goal is to identify your weak points so that the investigator will know how

Valentina Saveleva (b. 1954) was arrested in January 1982 while transporting Christian literature. Although it was her first arrest, authorities gave 27-year-old Valentina the unusually harsh sentence of five years' imprisonment. After the sentencing, virtually no news about her reached the West until her release in January 1987. She lives in Budennovsk with her mother, Yulia Pavlovna Saveleva.

to put pressure on you effectively, they pay great attention even to trivial details.

Those many months in the investigation cell were a
difficult time for me, but one very exciting thing happened there. I had asked the investigator to let me under-
take my own defense at the trial. He denied my request,
saying that I lacked specialized legal training. So I wrote
to the district prosecutor, asking that he allow me to
conduct my own defense and that, to prepare, I be given a
Bible and a copy of the Criminal Code. After several
discussions the investigator brought me a Bible—my
own Bible that had been confiscated!

When I saw it, the first thought that came to mind was
what the angel told Elijah when he was totally exhausted
and sleeping under the juniper tree. The angel tapped
him on the side, woke him up, and said, "Here's food and
water. Take it and be strengthened, because there's a very
long journey ahead of you." I realized then that the Lord
was giving me food for a long journey. I knew my sentence would not be short.

My Bible fascinated the other prisoners and the guards.
Whenever we were searched, the guards turned its pages
carefully and asked where I got it and how much I paid
for it. This was not just idle curiosity. These people were
seriously interested, because a Bible is hard to find in our
country.

Nobody bothered me when I knelt to pray in the cell,
and I could read the Bible freely. I often thought of those
words in the Twenty-third Psalm, "My cup runneth
over." My cup truly did run over, because the Lord had
prepared me a feast in full view of my enemies during
those days before the trial. Eventually the authorities
took the Bible away from me, saying that it had been

given to me illegally. But I refused to go to any interrogations until they returned it, so they gave it back to me in order for the investigation to be completed.

The investigator, too, was interested in the Bible. He especially wanted to read about the trial of Christ, so I found it for him.

"As you can see, history repeats itself," I remarked when he had finished reading.

"What do you mean?" he asked.

"Just as there were no grounds to condemn Christ to death, and his enemies had to find false witnesses, so you look for false witnesses against me. They said that he was acting against Caesar, and you say that my activities are against the government. Pilate washed his hands, saying that he found no guilt in Christ, but he handed him over for crucifixion anyway. You tell me, 'We're sorry this is happening to you,' but at the same time you promise me a five-year sentence."

At last the trial began in the Hall of Justice in Stavropol. After two days it was moved to the club at Krasnymetallist factory, where it continued for two days. The trial was open to the public, and word started getting around the city about who was on trial and where it was being held. Many curious spectators came, especially young people. Many of my Christian friends also came. During the first two days, believers had been able to get in with no problems, but toward the end of the trial they were crowded out. All the seats near the front were occupied by militant atheists.

All during the preliminary investigation, I had made it very clear that I wanted to defend myself. I would not accept a lawyer—because I was not allowed to have the one I wanted and did not need the help of a person who was obligated to do the court's bidding. However, in spite of my objections, the court still assigned a lawyer to me. I saw her for the first time in the courtroom. The woman was completely unfamiliar with my case. She didn't even know why I had been indicted for violation of certain articles of the Criminal Code. We were not allowed to confer before the trial, and during the whole process we were kept at a distance from one another. She was upset about all this and asked that she be released as my lawyer, saying that the whole process was degrading to her as a lawyer and as a person. However, the court forced her to defend me because she was being paid for it. I told the court that I rejected her as my lawyer because I could not entrust my defense to an atheist. Although she supported me in this, the court refused to allow any change. She was required to participate in the trial even though the judge and his assistants constantly interrupted her and refused to let her speak. She became indignant about the whole affair and at one point walked over to me and said, "I'm sorry; it doesn't seem that I can do anything for you."

"Don't worry," I answered. "I understand. They're going to give me five years, no matter what."

The judge and his assistants acted prejudiced against me, and it was clear that someone behind the scenes was directing the case. They were just following orders. At one point one of the judge's assistants told a witness that she could not possibly read the Bible herself because it is written in Old Church Slavonic. Obviously the judge's assistant did not even know that we have Bibles in Russian.

The state prosecutor's statements were often nothing more than attacks and accusations against believers. One day he said, "You claim that you haven't infringed on the rights of other citizens, but you pray on your knees. This is very degrading." Some of the workers and students applauded his statement.

"If kneeling is degrading to you," I answered, "no one forces you to do it. For me this is a sacred position of prayer. And if you bring this up in court as an accusation, I must answer that this isn't a legal accusation; rather it's public defamation. There is nothing criminal in kneeling to pray. It is the right of a believer, according to his own convictions. What's wrong is for you to use it as an excuse for public reproach." This time some of the audience applauded me.

When I made that statement, my lawyer also supported me. She told the prosecutor that he was spreading hostility and hatred on the grounds of religious belief. But in the end, as the KGB had threatened, the judge sentenced me to five years' imprisonment.

I decided to appeal the decision. However, I was immediately transferred to another cell, and all my documents remained in the previous one—the indictment, the portions I had copied from the Criminal Code, and all my notes. I wrote to the warden, asking that the documents be returned to me, but I was told that nobody knew anything about them and that no such documents existed. So I had to write the appeal from memory.

Two weeks later the appeal was returned to me. I realized that in such a short time my appeal could not have been sent to Moscow for review. Rather, it had been dealt with in Stavropol and then returned to me. The verdict stood unchanged.

On January 28 I was called up for prison transport, but not until I was actually on the train did I find out where I was being sent. I had expected to get assigned to the women's prison camp near my home. Instead, I was

being shipped to a camp near Irkutsk in Siberia. In one of
the transit prisons I wrote a note to the local warden,
asking on what grounds I was being sent to Siberia and
whether the order could be changed. He answered that
the order had come from Moscow and that only Moscow
could withdraw it.

The hardships of the prison transport were tremendous. We were freezing all the time, especially in the
prison vans and the small box cells for inmates who
arrived at night. These cells are unheated, and there is
nowhere to sit, so you have to stand or squat on the floor.
Since I had expected to be sent to the women's prison
camp near my home, I had no warm clothes with me.

The only food during transport was a little bread and a
small packet of sugar. I had no food with me for the trip,
but the Lord showed his mercy and softened the hearts of
the prisoners toward me. Once they found out what I was
sentenced for, these women became very concerned and
protective of me. They shared their food with me, and
the Lord gave me strength for the trip.

For a while I traveled with a woman who was being
taken to Kemerovskaya oblast. We used a little plastic
bag to hold sugar, and it was always about half full.
People kept giving us sugar, and we never ran out. This
experience reminded me of the widow of Zarephath who
fed Elijah. There was always enough—not more, not
less—and we had enough sugar to last through the whole
transport.

I was in the transit prison in Aktyubinsk for about a
week. The cell was built to hold ten, but there were
thirty women in it. People slept on the floor, under the
table, and even beside the latrine bucket. There was no
glass in the window, only a grill, so the prisoners had

stuffed pillows and rags between the bars, trying to block out the cold.

The worst conditions, however, were in the Irkutsk prison, the last prison before I reached the camp. I was in an old wing of the complex. My first cell was so crowded that there was not even room to sleep on the floor. Later they moved me to another cell, which was a little less crowded. There, too, the window had no glass in it, and a thick layer of frost coated all four walls. The warm breath of the prisoners melted the frost on the ceiling, causing it to drip on us day and night. It was impossible to get warm. We were there for four days before being loaded onto the train for the camp in Bozoi.

I heard a lot about this camp from the other prisoners. The camp was established in 1931 on the site of an abandoned cemetery and is known as "the valley of death" because of its high mortality rate. The climate is particularly severe, and there is a lot of tuberculosis. The village of Bozoi itself belongs to the Buryat people, who have a shamanistic faith and worship spirits. As the story goes, when the camp was first built, one of the local Buryat people warned, "People cannot live here. They will grow sick and die. You will never have a warden last long here." His prediction turned out to be right.

Finally, after over a month of the transport and transit prisons in Pyatigorsk, Aktyubinsk, Orenburg, Chelyabinsk, and Irkutsk, I arrived at the camp in Bozoi on March 3, 1983. The conditions were disheartening. To begin with, it was Siberia, very different from the European part of the Soviet Union, and it was such a desolate, remote spot. Bozoi is about one hundred kilometers from Irkutsk, and the villagers there say it is a region forsaken by God and man. Supplies for the camp were brought on horse-drawn carts.

The winds in Bozoi are very strong. My first summer was rainy; our jackets and heavy work boots were never dry. Often there was frost on the ground when we lined up for morning roll call. The camp had no asphalt, just dirt, so we stood in puddles during roll call and sometimes waded through knee-deep mud to get to work.

Getting clean again presented a whole new series of problems. The camp had been built to house 1,700 to 1,800 people but actually held around 3,000 women. The laundry was much too small for so many people. Since water had to be hauled into the camp in barrels, it was always in demand. And even when you could get water, you still had to find a basin to carry it. Prisoners would steal water from each other so as to have some to drink or wash with. Of course, there were no washers or dryers! Sometimes we could not bathe because there was no water or because there were problems with the baths, but the camp administration never cared whether we were clean or not.

Because the camp was so crowded, there were not enough bunks for everyone. People slept on the floor and in the corridors. For two years we had no heat in my barracks. The old wooden barracks with stoves were warm, but our barracks had central heating that did not work. So we dressed for bed the same way we dressed to go outside: we put on everything we owned. Often we had to cover ourselves with our mattresses in order not to freeze completely. At night I would wake up because my face and nose were freezing, so I would put my nose under the blanket to warm it up, then stick it out again to breathe. This would go on all night.

Everything in the barracks was frozen—sheets of ice

covered the windows, thick frost clung to the walls and ceiling. As in the Irkutsk prison, when the prisoners came back to the barracks at night to sleep, the warmth of their breath melted the frost on the ceiling, and it would start to drip. Because the beds were constantly damp, it was impossible to get warm. So everyone was glad to go to work: we could move around, and the work area was heated.

I was assigned to the section where material is cut out for sewing. Our working day was not a set number of hours. Instead, we worked until we had met our quotas. We started at 5:30 A.M. and often worked until 2:00 or 3:00 A.M. Then we would catch a few hours of sleep and return to work. There was very little mechanization, and the work was quite hard. But God very clearly impressed this truth on my heart: whatever God sends, whatever difficulties he allows, that is what will be. Before being sent to Bozoi, I had prayed that wherever God sent me, he would give me the strength to work. At first, things were very hard physically, but God preserved me in his mercy, through the prayers of my friends and the church.

My first official chat in the camp was with my work-brigade leader. Prison administrators watch Christians suspiciously. They don't know what to expect from us and are afraid of complaints, agitation, and refusal to work. The brigade leader made various threats, but the Lord gave peace to my heart. I told her, "I'm willing to drink the cup that the Lord has ordained for me. I've followed God willingly, and he'll give me strength."

As soon as I had arrived in the camp I let the warden know that I was a Christian and that I would not work on certain Christian holidays, like Christmas and Easter and Pentecost. I said that I was sentenced for my religious beliefs, not for any crime. I added, though, that I was not refusing to work; I would be willing to work on free days to make up for the work I missed on holidays. The administration was not sure what to make of this. They watched to see what I would do.

My first test came on Easter. I had not seen my family except for a brief fifteen minutes after the trial. I was expecting them to come to the camp for a scheduled visit and bring me some warm clothes, soap, shampoo, and other necessities. (I had not earned enough to buy anything in the camp store.) I knew that I might be punished for not working on Easter, and though not afraid of being put in the punishment cell, I was very concerned that I might be denied my visit with my family. As it turned out, the Lord took care of it completely. I was allowed to make up the work on another day, and I was also able to visit with my family. When I woke up on Easter morning, I greeted the whole barracks with the words "Christ is risen!" Many of them answered back, "He is risen indeed!"

Each Christian holiday, I took a day of rest. Then the Lord gave me the strength to do a double quota on another day, so the work didn't suffer, and none of the other prisoners were forced to do my work. I always tried to do as much work as I could and also to help the other women. There were many opportunities for me to help others, and because of this they were kind to me.

At first, however, the other prisoners were also suspicious of me. They do not look so much at what you were convicted for; they look at you personally and watch your every step. They notice how you treat people. If they grow to like you, they will take an interest in what you believe. They were interested in everything about me. The fact that I prayed raised many questions. "How do you pray?" they asked. "What do you pray about? And why do you get so many letters?" I gave them letters to read, and soon they started taking the initiative and asking to see them. They asked if they could have the bookmarks people sent with Bible verses, and they started asking me to tell them something from the Bible.

During holidays I would sometimes receive three or four hundred cards. The concern of my friends lifted my spirit tremendously and gave me great joy, which spilled over even to the other prisoners. They would come to me and ask, "How many cards did you get today? Why, that's more than yesterday!" They themselves kept count. The cards came at a rate of twenty to thirty per day. Between holidays, when there was less mail, the guards and prisoners would ask, "How come there's so little mail? Did your friends forget you already?" They followed my correspondence very closely and always wanted to see the letters.

Several women copied the poems and psalms in my letters and memorized them. One time something interesting happened. We generally had no time to sit around reading because all our time was taken up with work and sleep. One Christian friend sent me a letter containing Nikolai Melnikov's poem "The Rose and Barbed Wire." I gave it to a woman in the barracks to read, and she copied it. Not long after that I was working at my table when I heard a chorus of voices reciting together, "Letters from loved ones are withheld. . . ." I looked up and saw that at one of the workbenches the women were memorizing Melnikov's verses together. I was a little ashamed because there *they* were, memorizing the poem, yet I had managed to memorize so little of the poetry my friends sent to me. On another day a woman walked over and said, "I've learned to sing that hymn you gave me, 'Lord,

Teach Me to Pray.'" She had made up her own tune, but I
didn't try to teach her the original. I simply rejoiced that
she had learned it.

One very touching incident concerning my mail was
the arrival of a package at Easter from Christians in another country. According to the camp regulations, I was
due to receive a package, so I was summoned to the
office. But when the guards saw that the package was
from abroad they were unwilling to give it to me without
checking with the KGB.

"Who's it from?" they asked. "What's in it? You
should refuse to accept it." They told me to write a note
refusing it, saying that I didn't need it, and then return it
to the sender.

I answered that I had no intention of refusing it, that
since customs had cleared the package, I should be allowed to receive it. So they finally gave it to me. The
package contained a lovely warm, knit scarf. For me, it
was touching that these people had thought about me
there in Siberia, that they had prayed and sent this scarf
to keep me warm and protect me from illness. The Lord
used this and similar incidents to remind me constantly
that I had not been forgotten by my friends or the church
or even Christians in other countries.

I was also very touched to receive the letters of children who would sign their greetings "Nadia, age 7," or
"Natasha, age 8." With simple, childlike sincerity, they
tried to do their share in easing my situation. Already the
burdens and needs of the church had become the burdens
of their little hearts. The Lord had awakened sympathy
in them and was preparing them to have a part in ministering to God's people.

Sometimes friends would write and say, "We haven't
received any answer from you, and we don't know if

there's any point in writing. It seems the letters don't get through." But one friend thought of a solution to this problem. She decided to number her letters. I received #1, #3, and #10, but not the numbers in between. I was struck by this sister's firm faith. She wrote, "Whether you receive my letters or not, I'll continue writing to you. I'm doing this as a service to the Lord. I've made a commitment to write to you, and I'll keep writing." The Lord gave me such joyful fellowship with this woman.

All of the letters, of course, are read by censors, guards, and KGB agents, and I believe that the Word of God will not return empty. If there are some letters that I did not receive, they were read by others, and the Word of God will do its work in their hearts in time. The letters that I did receive I gave to others with the firm assurance that the Lord will do his work in their lives as well.

One Christmas Day I received from some friends in Omsk a letter with little fir twigs in it. I arranged the twigs on the table and suggested to another woman that we have a little celebration. I had some food from a parcel to share with her. She stood and listened very timidly while I prayed, but after that her attitude toward God changed completely. She started asking questions and even read my Scriptures for herself. Later she confided to me, "I thought believers were bad people. I was always told that Christians were criminals."

That was a Christmas I will never forget!

One of the most depressing aspects of camp life was the oppressive atmosphere of evil. The people around me were constantly cursing one another. There were periods when it seemed I could not pray, that the heavens were sealed up and silent. It was impossible to get alone. One time I was so anxious about my spiritual condition that I decided to go to one of the forbidden zones behind the buildings just to be alone and pray. But, as I headed in that direction, a guard spotted me and shouted for me to get back to work.

The Lord saw my need and in his mercy sent me a Christian sister named Natasha from Novokuznetsk. She is a wonderful Christian, of sterling character, full of peace, and it was evident that the Lord was with her. The Lord sent her to give me relief in my critical moment of need. We prayed together a lot and always tried to support one another in the arms of prayer. I remember how we often met outside at night under the open heavens. We couldn't stay there long, because the temperature was often below $-40°$ Fahrenheit and our work boots didn't keep our feet very warm. We would sing and pray for a few minutes, go back to our separate barracks to warm up a little, then meet outside again. Sometimes we stood silently, just gazing together toward heaven. Nothing was dearer to us than heaven.

The physical conditions in camp were so harsh that I was not at all sure I would survive. Sometimes my only desire was that the Lord would hurry up and take me home to be with him. But Natasha refreshed me very much. She had such a solid influence for good on my life. Often I thought that the Lord sent her to that camp just for my sake.

Whenever we received news of others who had been arrested, our hearts were filled with pain, and we would cry out to God, "O Lord, how long will your people be a sacrifice? Help your people, Lord." It was especially hard to hear about the men whose sentences were extended. I imagined what a heartbreak that must be. I knew for myself how hard it is when your strength is at an end. I had a secret desire—if only I could go home for a month, or even just a week, to see my friends, to be at just one worship service, and then to return to this place and these people. But the Lord has his own plans for each of us. He did not allow me to be released early, but he did allow me to have his Word. My heart overflowed with gratitude as he spoke to me through the Scriptures.

Natasha and I were also supported by the letters of friends. Evening mail call was always a time of celebration. We shared our letters with each other. It was particularly encouraging when the Lord used some verse of Scripture that someone included in a letter to encourage our hearts, to answer our questions, or to address a specific need. For instance, I had to work extremely long hours to meet my quota. At first I considered this work to be a burden. I compared myself to Samson. *How long, I wondered, will I have to turn these millstones?* But then some friends sent me a postcard with the verse, "And whatsoever ye do, do it heartily as to the Lord." The Lord showed me clearly that I should do my work and everything else in life in the name of the Lord and for the Lord. I had to ask for his forgiveness in this matter, and I asked him to enable me to do the work well and do it for him. The Lord gave me real victory in this, and he gave me such success and ability in my work that by the end of my term, by his mercy, I had become a production specialist! The supervisors in the work division even started turning to me with questions and asking for my help. I was glad to help them, of course, and because of this they liked me and respected me and treated me well.

During my years of imprisonment I prayed to God in many different places and situations. I knew that, wherever I was, the Lord was with me and he heard me. For a while I went out into the freezing cold late at night to pray with Natasha. Other times, when the prisoners were all going to sleep, I would kneel to pray. The need of my heart was just to be alone with God, to talk to him, to pour out my soul, to give him all my cares, and to thank him for his warm presence with me. And the Lord visited me in those hours of prayer.

I also prayed at the table before eating. I always stood and prayed quietly to myself. There was one woman, however, who didn't like my praying. I had often talked to her about the Lord, but she had not agreed with me. She was raised Orthodox and felt it was not necessary to change any of her views about God. But the Lord dealt with her in an interesting way. She had lower-back problems and developed a severe inflammation. When her condition grew worse, and she couldn't work, I helped her as much as I could. I practically did her work for her, helped her to dress, and brought her food. She would look at me with tears in her eyes because in camp everyone usually thinks only of herself. If a person gets sick, nobody needs her, and she is left completely alone. Most people have only the strength to look after their own needs, and it is very hard to carry another person's burdens. So, when a Christian takes on another person's burden, this really makes an impression on other people. I think this is the greatest possible sermon in camp; to do good to others in the name of the Lord. In turn, the Lord gave me strength to do my own work and also to help this woman.

When the woman's situation got critical and she became completely helpless, I suggested that we pray for healing. I believe the Lord put this desire in my heart. She stood with me, and we prayed. I called on the Lord, and she stood beside me in great distress, crying and maybe praying quietly to herself. When I finished, she said, "Amen." After we prayed about her back, the Lord sent her relief, and she started getting better. She said to me, "You don't have to tell me anything else because I know that God has healed me." For the rest of her term this woman had no more back problems, even though in freedom she had always suffered attacks of pain in the spring and the fall. There in the camp, after the Lord had healed her, she began to pray and started taking an interest in the Word of God. Whenever we were together at meals, she would ask me to pray aloud. She would stand beside me and at the end say "Amen" in front of everyone.

Another woman I talked to quite a bit started reading the Word of God and praying, and sometimes we would pray together. It was precious to hear her thank God for sending one of his children to her in bonds. She said, "Lord, you sent Valentina here for me, and I thank you for her!" Prayers like this strengthened my own trust in the Lord and filled my heart with gratitude that the Lord has a purpose for sending his children where he sends them.

There had been a certain period in the camp when nobody showed much interest in God, and no one asked any questions about him. During this time one woman said to me, "What's the purpose of your ministry here? There's no point. Everything you're doing is futile!"

"Even if no one is interested," I answered, "I'm content to be here just to pray for these people and to be a reminder of God's mercy and longsuffering and his call to repentance."

The Lord led other people my way, people he wanted me to talk to, and I believe that he will continue to lead them to me. Seeds of the gospel were planted in many people's lives. May the Lord grant that the seeds will grow and that more people will come to know him.

There were, of course, those who for one reason or

another were working with the KGB. I had already encountered this situation in the prison. The authorities
were putting together a detailed psychological portrait of
me. The questions asked by the brigade leader, the KGB
agents, and others were very specific, designed to give a
clear picture of a person's character and personality. Apparently this is done for future use so that the KGB will
know how to approach a person and work on him or her. I
got the impression that the KGB puts together such a file
on each Christian and that it follows the Christian from
freedom to prison camp and then back to freedom.

In answer to several of the questions that KGB agents
put to me, I said, "It sounds as if you've already consulted
with the KGB in my home town."

They laughed and answered, "Yes, we've talked to
them already."

So I replied, "In that case, there's no point in talking
further. You don't need to ask the same questions twice."

Throughout my five-year term, the authorities observed me, studied me, tried to determine my weak-
nesses and to bend me. Sometimes they offered
privileges and special conditions. For example, there was
the matter of short visits. My family was in no position
to fly all the way to Siberia for the two-hour visit due me,
so the camp officials allowed some Christian friends
from Irkutsk to come instead. After the first visit,
though, the KGB started to impose conditions. They said
they would allow me another visit with Christians from
Irkutsk only if I would persuade them to be more loyal to
the authorities. I refused, of course, and said, "No, thank
you; I don't need a visit. I'm fine." This made them really
angry, and they mocked, "We can see that you're fine.
Everything's just great." But the Lord gave me strength to
stand firm.

Another time the KGB were very interested in my personal morality and my relationships with other people. For instance, they wanted to find out if I was likely to betray others, so they suggested that I work for the KGB in the camp, reporting on other prisoners. They even asked me if I had any complaints against the camp administration. This was one of their main tactics: to try to get me to complain about life in camp. The devil seems to believe that if he can make a person sin in this way, he will gain mastery over that person's soul. They offered to move me to a camp closer to home if I would cooperate, but I refused, saying, "If I needed anything from you, I would've agreed long ago and wouldn't have gotten this five-year term in the first place." Then they offered to let me study at the state university in the philosophy department, saying I had the ability for it. I knew this flattery was just another tactic, and I answered, "Thank you, but I've already finished four years of college."

In addition to asking me questions, the KGB watched carefully to see how I behaved in camp. They wanted to know my very thoughts, to see if I was growing weak. Once they said, "What's wrong with you? When you first came, you used to smile more often. Are you getting weak already?" But the Lord used even these words to encourage me. I learned to see the hand of God in everything, everywhere. I learned to constantly recognize and experience God's mercy and rejoice in it.

The KGB also wanted to know who wrote to me, and they were interested in seeing the letters that I wrote. They especially wanted to know what things were particularly hard for me, in order to aggravate my condition and so break my spirit and gain control over me. Whenever I received letters, the officers asked the other women in the barracks, "What was her reaction to the

letters? Which ones upset her? Which ones made her
happy?" I became aware that several people were writing
reports on me. Records are kept of all the re-educational
work done with each prisoner. I learned from a reliable
source that the reports on me were compiled and up-
dated every three months, sometimes even more fre-
quently. They included reports from my brigade leader,
the officials in charge of the work section, and many
others.

One civilian official in particular summoned me a
number of times for discussions, and I was able to find
out what he wrote about me. He reported that over the
course of several years he had conducted a number of
conversations with me on various questions and topics.
He said that he had determined my level of knowledge
and my views on various subjects, and he concluded that
the general direction of my life was proper and whole-
some—with the exception of my religious views. He included a notation that, in spite of the fact that I had
completed only an intermediate level of specialized education, I was very keen and incisive, quick to refute arguments, and able to support my arguments logically by
quoting the Bible. In conclusion, he predicted that at the
end of my term I would return to my religious activities.
Obviously the KGB had various sources—prisoners and
civilian officials—but the informants did not know each
other.

I greeted 1987 still in bonds. On the eve of the new
year, I gathered several of the women to whom I was
closest, and we had a time of fellowship. We had saved
some food for this occasion. After we ate, they asked me
to tell them the story of Christmas. Then several of them
asked questions about the life of Christ. In conclusion I
recited some poems and gave them some special New

Year's wishes. But then they asked me to tell them something more. Normally I would have given them bookmarks, but I had none left. Then the Lord put in on my heart to give them each a verse from Psalm 119. I suggested that each woman pick a number and I would read the corresponding verse. "May you accept it as a gift from the Lord," I said, "as a guide for the new year." And when I read the verses, they were all delighted, saying, "My, that verse suits me exactly!"

Before my release on January 23, I was summoned by the KGB. They asked me a whole series of questions and wanted to know if I had changed my convictions. Each time they asked this, I asked back, "What should I change them to?" They could never offer anything in exchange, so that question fell by the wayside. Finally they asked, "How will the authorities receive you when you get home?"

"The way they receive me will be determined by the file and the psychological portrait you send them," I answered.

Then they started to laugh and said, "Okay, we can see what's going on here. You may go."

I parted on good terms with my fellow prisoners. Many thanked me for the cards I had given them, for my prayers and support, and just for sharing in their lot. Most of the guards and administrators also said good-bye to me. I was taken to the gate at 9:00 A.M., just as they were coming to work, and they all said good-bye, wished me the best, and told me not to come back again because that place was not for me! They realized that believers are not criminals, and the Lord had disposed their hearts kindly toward me. I remembered the Scripture verse that says that when a man's ways please the Lord, he makes

even his enemies to be at peace with him. This was
another way that the Lord showed his mercy to me.

The camp warden assigned one of the guards to drive
me to the regional center in his own car because there are
no buses from the camp. Perhaps his motive was not just
to be kind, but to get me away from the camp and away
from Bozoi as quickly as possible so that none of my
friends from Irkutsk could meet me at the camp and sing
and take pictures.

All during my term, people asked me, "Don't you regret the time that you're wasting here?" The investigator
had asked me this question while I was in prison before
the trial, and guards and prisoners asked the same question in camp. The Lord put it on my heart to answer
them in different ways, but the main idea was always the
same: "If the Son of God willingly raised his arms on the
cross for me, what in comparison is five years of my
earthly life?"

Some people might also say, "You could do more in
freedom. You can believe whatever you want, but just
learn to be flexible, to compromise. The church needs
you; you'll be more fruitful at home. Why should you be
here in prison camp?"

But the Lord gave me assurance that my five-year journey was before his eyes. The ministry he gave me in the
prison camp was the work he wanted me to do. I am sure
that if I had compromised in order to be released early,
the Lord would not have given me such peace of conscience and joy and, most importantly, I would not have
gained precious heavenly treasure.

During my five years in bonds, I often thought of Ro-
mans 8:37: ". . . in all these things we are more than
conquerors through him that loved us." Only by God's
mercy was I able to walk in his way, to do the work he

After her return home, Valentina is still smiling.

Valentina with her church youth group.

gave me to do, and to exalt his name before the prisoners and guards. Sometimes I lacked even the strength to pray; I could only raise my eyes to heaven in a silent cry. The Lord, however, is very loving and compassionate in the help he gives his people. Through his strength—not my own—I, too, was able to stand firm and be more than a conqueror for him.

3

Vladimir Rytikov
Cellmate of a False Christ

In the summer of 1979, my father and Galina Vilchinskaya and I helped to gather more than thirty children together for Bible camp in Zakarpatia. Most of them were children of prisoners, and some of their fathers were already serving a second or third prison term. Our goal was to enrich the children spiritually with the living Word of God and also to get them rested and strengthened for the upcoming school year.

On the way home from the camp, we three were met by policemen at the Lvov train station at six o'clock in the morning. "A man was killed on the train and his

Vladimir Rytikov (b. 1959) was just 20 when police arrested him in August 1979, together with his father (Pavel) and another Christian, Galina Vilchinskaya, for teaching children's Bible classes. Since his release, Vladimir has been forced to conduct much of his ministry while in hiding. He was married in 1984 to Luda Yudintsev, the sister of another former prisoner for the gospel, Andrei Yudintsev (see chapter 1).

things were stolen," they explained. "Suspicion has fallen on you, and we're taking you to the police station."

They grabbed our arms and led us away. We were held several hours. Then KGB Major Malyshev arrived, saying he was "Police Major Statsenko." He had us moved to another station, where we waited until eleven o'clock at night, when a warrant was finally brought for our arrest. Then we were sent to another jail, where we were held for a month.

During that month, the investigator and a KGB agent questioned each of us individually. Then they wrote up reports containing false statements about our churches and tried to force me to sign them. So I stopped answering their questions altogether and would not sign the reports or say that I was guilty. I would give no information at all! In response to their shouts and threats, I tried to maintain a prayerful composure. At one point, Malyshev (alias Statsenko) said to me, "Do you want to be a hero of the faith like Vanya Moiseyev? We can help you with that!"

Informers dressed like prisoners often tried to draw information out of us for the KGB, to listen for some slip-up in conversation. One time I was lying on my bunk, and a new prisoner was brought into the cell. He was of average height, with long hair and a beard. He looked just the way Jesus is always shown in pictures. After talking with some of the other prisoners, he sat down near me and asked, "Are you a believer?"

"Yes," I answered, watching him carefully.

"You believe in God? You believe in Christ?"

"Yes, I do."

"I am Christ," he said, and then he started telling me all sorts of stories from the Bible by memory. He had an excellent knowledge of the Bible.

"Very soon I will judge the world," said the newly appeared "Christ" in a conspiratorial tone. "The first time, I came to save people, but now I have come for judgment."

"How can you be Christ?" I said. "Christ is coming in glory. He won't come in the form of a man as he did the first time."

"But this is how I have come, just as you see me!"

"How can you say you're Christ when you use such foul language? And your life, as you've described it, is full of sin."

"I don't use foul language when I talk to you. But I do swear when I speak to unbelievers. Don't you remember how I drove the buyers and sellers out of the temple with a whip? I was angry with them! I only swear and show my wrath to unbelievers."

I tried to ignore him. I got up and started walking around the cell, singing to myself, "Oh, love of Christ, boundlessly great. . . ."

He walked up to me and said, "You're singing about me." He tried to learn the words and sing along.

Once when the men in Papa's cell were taken out to the exercise yard, I climbed up to the window. The man calling himself Christ also climbed up. He imitated all my movements, mimicked every gesture.

I called out the window, "Papa, this man says he's Christ and that he's come to judge the world!"

The next day I climbed up to the window again. So did the other man. "Papa," I called, "how can he be Christ when he swears and uses foul language? He's a false christ!"

"That's exactly what he is," Papa called back. "He's a false christ!" After that the man stopped bothering me.

About a month later, Papa, Galina, and I were moved

to another prison. When I stepped into my cell, I said, "Peace to this house!"

The prisoners answered, "We welcome you in peace!" They were eager to talk. They asked questions about my faith, about God, and asked which article of the Criminal Code I was indicted under. When I explained, many were surprised and indignant. "How can this be? You've been put in prison for your faith in God? We don't have any laws against faith!"

I was in that cell for about two months. In the beginning, the other prisoners treated me very well. But then the investigator and KGB Agent Malyshev came to the prison and started summoning the prisoners and stirring them up against us, saying we only pretended to be believers, that we had been arrested in the station carrying knives, which we used to attack passengers and force them to believe in God. The attitude of the prisoners began to change. They came back from these talks and yelled, "You lie when you say you're a believer! You're just anti-Soviet!"

At first I tried to explain, but I found that it was pointless. After that I just tried to keep quiet. At night when I was sleeping, the other prisoners would throw boots at me or douse me with cold water.

At one point I was moved to a cell for three people. The other man in the cell had been arrested for bribery, and in the prison he worked as an informer. His behavior toward me was indecent. He did all kinds of disgusting things to me, like spitting in my food. He tried to draw information out of me for the investigator, but he never succeeded. I was with him for six months.

The investigation dragged on for a year. Senior Investigator Shemchuk from the prosecutor's office in Lvov often came to interrogate me. He threatened to send me to a psychiatric hospital. One time when he called me into his office, his eyes were bloodshot, and he was foaming at the mouth. He grabbed a sharp pen and lunged at me. He waved the pen in front of my eyes and under my chin and with the other hand shoved documents in my face, demanding that I sign them.

The Lord, however, granted me peace in my heart, and the threats did not upset me. My composure infuriated Shemchuk. "You're a psychopath!" he screamed. "Just wait! We'll lock you up in a psychiatric hospital!"

In my next cell noxious fumes poured through the broken windows. One other prisoner was brought in. The smoke in the cell was so dense that we could not even see the light. Everything was in a fog. There was no air to breathe. We pounded on the door, calling for the guards to move us or cover the windows, but they paid no attention.

Every day the investigator summoned me for questioning and asked, "How's your head? Does it hurt? Get ready for the psychiatric hospital!"

My head did hurt from the fumes, and I was nauseated. With the Lord's help, I was able to send a letter out of the prison to my family. Within a week, Mama came to the prison and talked to the investigator.

Then the prison warden summoned me. He was amazed. "How in the world did your mother know what's happening to you here?"

Then Knischuk, the head of the operative division, started screaming at me and using the foulest language. "Just wait until you get to the camp! I'll take care of you there!"

Finally, after over a year in prison, Papa, Galina, and I were brought to court. The trial lasted three days. We were accused of traveling from city to city, persuading people not to send their children to school but rather to teach them religion. I objected that we had never done any such thing. Since we were not guilty, our accusers could present no convincing evidence against us. But the regional court convicted us anyway. We were each sentenced to three years' imprisonment.

In November 1980 I was told to collect my things and get ready for transport. I was driven to the train station and loaded onto a prison car. Galina and I were put on the same train. We traveled several days to reach Kharkov. My father was left in Lvov for two more weeks.

From Kharkov we traveled three days to Sverdlovsk. In the Kharkov prison the Lord had granted us a special blessing. We met our friends Tamara Bystrova and Sergei Bublik, who had been arrested for working with a printing team and were being taken from the Dnepropetrovsk prison to camp, Sergei to Krasnoyarsky krai and Tamara to Chelyabinsk. It was a very joyful meeting. We prayed that the Lord would grant us another meeting, in the camp or somewhere along the way, wherever he saw fit. And the Lord did grant our desire: Sergei and I traveled in neighboring train cars, and Tamara and Galina were together.

When we reached the Sverdlovsk prison, Sergei and I were put in the same cell! We embraced and cried and thanked the Lord that he had preserved us. We encouraged and comforted each other. I was with Sergei for four days, and we sang, quoted Bible verses, and prayed that the Lord would protect the workers of the Christian Publishing House.

The Sverdlovsk prison is a horrible place. It is the central transfer prison in Russia. We noticed that the walls were red, but at first did not understand why. But when we lay down on the bunks, we saw that the walls were literally crawling with hordes of bugs that dropped down on us, biting us mercilessly.

Our cell was badly overcrowded. It was meant to hold thirty men, but actually held one hundred and twenty. Prisoners came in tired and threw themselves wherever they could. Not only was there no room to lie down, there was barely room to stand.

On the fifth day I had to part with my dear friend Sergei, who remained in Sverdlovsk. I was taken to Novosibirsk, then Irkutsk. The entire trip from Lvov to the Irkutsk prison took a month. By the time we got there, it was December. The transport cell in Irkutsk was crowded and cold, with no glass in the window and no place to sit. It was so frigid that I could not stand still.

On December 2, I finally arrived at my final destination—the labor camp in the city of Tulun. A young Adventist there who had been convicted for his beliefs was very kind to me. He gave me some felt boots and a padded jacket. He also had a Bible. I had not held this Holy Book in my hands for more than a year, so he gave it to me for a whole month! How I feasted on the precious Word of God!

Many prisoners asked me why I had been sentenced. When I told them, they were surprised and indignant to find out that Christians are imprisoned in our country. But some just didn't believe me. During those days I had many opportunities to talk about the Lord and the love of Christ.

In January Mama came for my scheduled visit. However, on the very day she arrived, the barracks were supposedly put under quarantine. During a real quarantine, prisoners are not allowed out of the barracks without a guard, and day workers are not allowed into the camp. But on this occasion people kept coming and going as

usual—only my mother was kept out! She decided to
stay in Siberia for two months, waiting for the quarantine to be lifted. She wrote me often from Krasnoyarsk.
During all this time my younger brothers and sisters
were left in the care of our ninety-year-old grandmother.

That first half year in the camp, I worked in a sawmill
and earned a grand total of four and a half rubles. Then
they stopped bringing wood to the camp, and there was
no work.

One day KGB Agent Petrov showed up and summoned
me to the office. "Things are easier for Christians here in
Siberia than in the Ukraine where you're from," he said.
"Listen, you can help us. Write a letter to your Christian
friends. Persuade them to register the church. If you help
us, we'll send you to a better camp, or maybe even release
you early."

Petrov summoned me three times before finally realizing that I was not going to cooperate. Then the authorities started locking me in the punishment cell. The
first time, I was put there for five days, supposedly for not
staying with my work brigade, even though I never left
my brigade.

When my mother arrived for our next scheduled visit,
I was sent to the punishment cell for fifteen days. When I
found out she was at the camp, I refused to eat; so they
finally let me out and allowed me to see her.

After Mama's visit, the days passed slowly. Then, on
May 5, three months before my release date, I was summoned and told that I had thirty minutes to collect my
things and get ready for transport. I managed to get my
photographs and my notebook of Bible verses before they
took me to a special prison in Tulun, where I was put in a
tiny cell. The window was pretty big, and not only was
there no glass, but there was not even a frame. I couldn't

lie down at night because it was unbearably cold, just as cold in the cell as on the street, and in May it can get bitterly cold in Siberia.

The next day I was summoned to the warden's office. When I entered, I saw KGB Captain Petrov. The warden started questioning me about my faith and about God, and he asked what article in the Criminal Code I was sentenced under. Suddenly he blurted, "Why did you separate from the AUCECB in 1961? Why won't you join with the registered churches?"

"In 1961 I was two years old," I answered.

"Are you trying to say that you're innocent in this matter?"

He ordered an officer to take me back to my cell. When I entered, I saw three other prisoners.

The officer asked them, "Is a week enough?"

"It's enough," they answered.

The door slammed shut.

The three prisoners, all of them big, husky men, started questioning me very directly about my faith and about life in the camp.

"Why are you suffering for nothing?" they asked. "After all, you're so young. Just write a statement to the KGB that you renounce your faith, and they'll let you go today! They'll give you the best apartment and anything you want. When you have a son, he'll become a cosmonaut. . . ." And on and on.

When I remained silent, they began shouting and threatening me. "We'll grind you into the cement! We'll punish you like a dog! We'll force you to renounce your faith!"

One of them kicked me in the shoulder, shouting, "Where's your God? Why doesn't he help you when I kick you? Why doesn't he hold my leg? If he exists, why doesn't he defend you? And you still believe in him? You serve him?"

"You say you're a Christian," said another, "so we'll carve the word *Christian* on your forehead. That way wherever you go people will see that you're a Christian! And we'll carve blasphemies on your back. Then how will you be a believer? What god will help you then?"

Not knowing what they might do to me, I prayed and asked the Lord for only one thing—that I might remain faithful to him to the end.

The next two days were filled with shouts and threats. On May 9, a Sunday, I decided to spend the day in prayer and fasting. At six o'clock in the morning, the three men were already up, making knives. They worked on them all day, sharpening and sharpening until they were drenched in sweat. They stopped only long enough to eat.

I was prepared for death. "Lord," I prayed, "if they attack me, let me be faithful to you to the end!" I thought about the early Christians who were tortured for their faithfulness to the Lord. I also thought of the martyrs of our own day, Khmara, Biblenko, Odintsov, Vanya Moiseyev, and others who had been tortured and killed. I was ready to meet the Lord and these others who had gone ahead of me into eternity. I no longer expected to see my friends again in freedom. I entrusted everything to the hands of the Lord.

When the bell rang for prisoners to go to bed, the other three men threw down their knives and literally collapsed onto their bunks from exhaustion. Then one of them got up and approached my bunk. He sat near me and said, "I love children. I want you to promise me that when you have children, you won't teach them religion. You have to promise right now. Otherwise, do you see that club in the corner? I'll beat you with that club as long as I'm in this cell."

"Do you think I'm afraid of that club?" I asked, ready not only for a beating, but even for death.

He was silent for a few minutes, then changed the subject. He talked to me like that all night.

The next day I was moved to another cell and then taken back to the camp. They put me in isolation for fifteen days, ostensibly because I had photographs in my possession. Of course, the camp administration had known for a long time that I had those photographs; they just wanted an excuse to punish me. After two weeks, guards took me out and beat me with clubs. Then they moved me around from cell to cell to make the other prisoners suspicious of me, to turn them against me.

Shortly before my release date, a guard came to get me and said, "Your family's here." He led me toward the visiting room, then suddenly gave me a shove that sent me stumbling forward into the zone forbidden to prisoners. He immediately took me to the punishment cell.

"On what grounds?" I objected.

"You know perfectly well!" he answered.

Then he started beating me and kicking me. He looked around for something to hit me with but couldn't find anything, so he kept using his hands and feet. The camp administration did not try to hide the fact that KGB agent Petrov was directing all of these illegal actions against me. Near the end of my sentence I mentioned it to Petrov.

"You don't like it here in the camp?" Petrov snarled. "I'll send you to the end of the earth! You just watch and see what I can do to you!" Then he ordered the head of the operative division to put me back in the punishment cell.

Vladimir Rytikov and his bride Ludmila Yudintseva (left) with Natasha Rytikova and her groom Vasily Dmitriev (right) were an unusual sight in the waiting room of this prison camp. Their father, Pavel Rytikov, had missed the double wedding ceremony of his children because he was still a prisoner. The children were permitted to visit with their father for an hour.

Just outside the prison camp in Komissarovka, Ukraine, Vladimir is waiting for a hug from his newly released father.

"But he has only five days left before his release!"

"I don't care! Lock him up!" Petrov insisted.

But I was not locked in the punishment cell after all. Instead, Officer Golovichev from the operative division just said to me, "If you get out of Tulun alive, you were born lucky!"

Finally the last day of my term arrived, August 23. At six o'clock in the morning, Golovichev and the camp warden came to the barracks to get me and took me to the gate. They wanted to send me away early so that my family could not greet me as I walked to freedom. But my family and friends were already there waiting.

Finally I was free! We all went to the home of an elderly Christian lady who lived nearby. Together we thanked the Lord for his mercy and care. But we could not even do this in peace! A policeman showed up, accused us of organizing an unauthorized meeting, and wrote up a report.

A couple of weeks later, on September 12, a wedding at our church in Krasnodon also served as a homecoming service for Papa and me. The church received us with such love! They had waited and prayed for us. And the Lord had heard their prayers and preserved us.

Today, when I think back on my time of imprisonment—the cold, gloomy Lvov prison, the camp, all the difficulties and trials, the hopelessness I sometimes felt—I want to thank all the people of God for their prayers and especially for remembering me on Fridays, the day of prayer and fasting, when I experienced a special awareness of the Lord's help. And I want to thank my God for the path by which he led me and for his strength, which enabled me, "having done all, to stand" (Eph. 6:13).

As Psalm 124 says, "If it had not been the LORD who

was on our side, when men rose up against us: Then they had swallowed us up quick, when their wrath was kindled against us" (vv. 2–3). Yes, if it were not for the Lord, who goes before his church and leads us by his mighty hand through all adversities, the world would really have destroyed the people of God long ago. But our help is in the name of the Lord. Glory to his name!

4

Pyotr Rumachik
The Richest Prisoner of All

For me, life as a prisoner was quite hard in 1981 and a large part of 1982 and 1983, but the year 1984 was a year of especially great trials. In that year my mail was stopped. I was told that I would not be allowed to send any more letters because my wife was spreading them around the country. So this door of communication was slammed shut. I could write back to no one, but could only give thanks in my prayers for the letters I received.

Then, at one point, I was put in the hospital for a long

"I personally had no hope that I would ever return home," said Pyotr Rumachik (b. 1931) of his most recent prison term. At age forty-nine, Rumachik faced his fifth imprisonment for the gospel, following his arrest in August 1980. A gifted preacher and vice president of the CEBC, Pastor Rumachik suffered unusually brutal treatment at the hands of Soviet authorities. Before his fifth term even ended, he was resentenced to yet another five years. Rumachik, the senior pastor of the independent Baptist church in Dedovsk, a Moscow suburb, was unexpectedly freed in February 1987. He and his wife, Lubov, have six children.

time and was so sick that I could barely breathe. Other prisoners carried me to the window for fresh air. I was so certain that I would die that in my prayers I said farewell to my family and my brothers and sisters in Christ. Later, the men who were with me there said, "We had no hope that you would survive."

I experienced times of imprisonment in the punishment cells, in concrete and iron, sometimes in crowded cells, sometimes in solitary confinement. All of this was very hard and certainly gave no comfort to the outer man. But, through it all, the Lord gave me strength to endure and "be of good cheer," as the apostle Paul put it.

In the hard times I spent many days in prayer and fasting before the Lord. I suppose those days would add up to weeks. Sometimes I got hardly any sleep for up to fifteen days, because the guards would keep me in cells where the windows had been knocked out, and I was shivering all the time. After one such spell I ended up in the hospital. As I said, this was a great hardship for the physical man, but the inner man was strengthened and comforted by God. During those long periods of prayer and fasting in solitary confinement, my heart enjoyed the presence of God. Like the apostle Paul, I would spend hours singing hymns.

The men in the next cells listened to me sing. I would call out, "Do you like these songs? Do you want me to sing some more?"

"Yes, keep singing. We've never heard such songs before. If you have strength, sing some more," they would answer.

Many of these men were criminals. They had done all sorts of terrible things. But the Lord softened their hard, black hearts. As I had opportunities to talk to them, some repented. The Lord sowed his seed in their hearts;

and there, in those very hard circumstances, people were saved. Sometimes people tried to keep me from talking about Christ, but the Lord again showed his mighty hand, and those whose hearts had already received the message stood by me. They were able to influence others, and through them the Lord gave a greater opportunity to witness about Christ.

When my circumstances were extremely hard, I was more aware than ever that my brothers and sisters in Christ were praying for me. I could feel their prayers. I knew that the church was not indifferent to me and the other Christians in bonds, but rather was crying out to the Lord on our behalf. I knew this with certainty even during periods when I was in isolation and received no mail.

There were other times, though, especially before holidays, when I received thirty to fifty letters a day, and telegrams as well. The young people sent so many bright, colorful, beautiful cards. I was the happiest, richest man. God's children poured out their souls in the letters, and I knew that the church was alert and praying. Many men in the camp never received any mail at all from family or friends. When they saw how much mail I received, they would say to me, "You're the richest man among us." Sharing my letters with them was always a wonderful opportunity for me. The other prisoners were surprised to read the greetings from people who had such deep compassion for those who suffer. Never in their lives had they heard of such care. The letters and cards provided a natural opening to talk to these people about Christ, his truth, his love for sinners, and his compassion for those who have been forsaken and forgotten by everyone else.

Many men asked me, "When we leave, will we be able to hear the Word of God somewhere?"

"Of course," I answered. "Just don't let God's Word depart from your heart. Anywhere you go, you'll be able to find God's people. Tell them what happened to you while you were in bonds. Tell them you know me, and they'll help you. They'll give you God's Word. Just keep seeking God; seek him, his truth, and his ways. Keep seeking that salvation that he offers to every man."

Amazingly, I was able to keep my Bible from 1980 up to February of 1987. It has been in many places, including solitary-confinement cells. A number of times the authorities took it away, once for more than a year, but the Lord returned it to me. Whenever I got it back, my joy was indescribable. Sometimes I knew that within a few hours or days they would take my Bible away again, so I would read chapter after chapter, whole books, in the semi-darkness of my cell, feeding on the Heavenly Bread that gave life to my soul and, through me, to others.

Once the guards tried to steal my Bible. They searched my cell and one of them secretly sneaked the Bible out in his pocket.

"Where did you get that Bible, anyway?" the old warden demanded when he got my complaint.

"I was given permission to have it, so either you or one of your subordinates must know where I got it," I answered.

After threatening to lock me in solitary, he finally gave it back. Then, for the next forty minutes, he asked me all kinds of questions about God. At the end of our talk, as I was leaving his office, he slapped me on the shoulder and said, "I guess I don't have many years left myself."

"That's all the more reason you should think about your soul. Otherwise, you may end up a most unfortunate man." Thus we parted.

During one of the times I was without my Bible, I was

writing a letter to my family when another prisoner walked over and held out a notebook to me. "Here, read this poem," he said.

"I'm right in the middle of a letter," I said. "If you'll let me keep it, I'll look at it as soon as I'm finished."

He realized that I was not really in the mood to look at his notebook, but he insisted, "Please, just read this one poem."

Looking up, I couldn't believe what I saw. There was a poem by Vera Kushnir about Christ's sufferings on Calvary. My spirit was strengthened and revived as I read it. I started flipping the pages, discovering other poems and some passages from Scripture, altogether 140.

The man stood to the side, watching and smiling as I turned the pages. "It's yours. You can keep it," he announced.

After I finished my letter, I spent the rest of the evening poring over the notebook. It was full of beautiful verses about Christ and the church, about how Christ calls the church his beloved, encourages us, and never forsakes the prisoners.

That notebook stayed with me for years and was especially precious during those times when I did not have my Bible. I managed to keep it through many searches, and I had hoped to bring it home with me, but last September the authorities took it away, supposedly to examine it, and in spite of all my pleas they didn't give it back.

So who was the man who gave me that notebook? He was far from being a Christian. He is one of the Buryat people from Zabaikal, descendants of the Mongols. The Buryat people know almost nothing of Christ. Some of them are religious people, Buddhists. The man who gave me the notebook, though, was not a Buddhist. He said that though he did not really believe in God, he used to listen to Christian radio programs late at night when he was shepherding. He taped the programs onto cassettes and later copied parts of them into the notebook. Somehow he managed to hang on to the notebook and get it into the camp.

I often compare this man to the raven that brought food to the prophet Elijah in the wilderness. People might say, "What good could a raven bring?" But, like the raven, this unbelieving man brought me food from the Lord, and for a long time I fed on the notebook that he had written with his own hand. God heard the prayers of his child and answered them in this amazing way.

In addition to the hardships and suffering that were my lot, the enemies also devised evil against my family, my wife in particular. KGB agents came to my camp and told me that she would soon be imprisoned, as soon as our youngest son was nine. Then letters stopped coming. For a long time I did not know where she was or how the children were. But I believed in the prayers of God's people. When I finally received a letter from home, I opened it and saw that the evil plans of the authorities had not been carried out.

But this was not the end of their threats against my wife. Because I was rearrested in the camp and resentenced, I was not able to come home at the end of my term. On December 2, 1985, the investigator told me that materials on my case also contained an accusation against my wife and that a case would be brought against her. But the Lord established a limit to what they could do. When I was brought to court on the first day of the trial, I didn't see my wife. Was she in prison? Had she been tried and sentenced? The second day she was still not there. But, on the third day, she came and was there for the rest of the trial. The Lord had heard my prayers and protected my wife.

The year 1986 became a time of solitary confinements and crowded, gloomy cells where I could see the sun and sky for only an hour a day. People were constantly smoking, and there was no fresh air to breathe. But God preserved me and gave me the strength to endure.

At the end of the year there was another long transport, and I was taken back to the Urals. I went through many hard experiences there, but at the end of December the situation became absolutely terrible. I cannot even describe my condition. From a human point of view, there was no help, no defense. I was receiving no letters at all. I knew that friends were writing, but all I received were reports saying that letters from such and such people had been confiscated because of "suspicious contents." What they meant by "suspicious" I don't know. I could find no one who would tell me. The purpose of the atheists' whole program is to beat a man down psychologically, to reduce him to despair.

On January 5 I expected to be put in the punishment cell, and at five o'clock in the morning, after breakfast, I was summoned. The duty officer said that a report had been written up against me for praying in the morning and that I would be put in isolation. On that same day I was supposed to see the warden, and I hoped that he might intervene on my behalf, but he would not even listen to me.

"The officer made the right decision, and I'll see to it that you're put in isolation today," he said. But, for some reason, that did not happen.

A week later I was denied a parcel and use of the

commissary as punishment for praying, but nothing further came of it. I accepted my punishment and was ready for anything that might happen. My spirit was unbroken. I was of good cheer, rejoicing and thanking the Lord for everything, even though, from my human perspective, it was impossible to foresee any change in my situation.

From January 14 to January 20, every day the pressure seemed greater, and I felt I was being crushed. But somehow I had hope in my heart. I remember sharing my thoughts with Vasily, a new brother in Christ, and he said, "I have a very definite feeling that you'll soon be free."

"Where did you get that idea?" I asked.

"Just wait and see, and remember what I said," he responded.

On January 20, at the end of the day, an officer summoned me and told me to change out of my work clothes as quickly as possible. He would answer none of my questions until we were out of the work zone, and then he said, "We're going to the barracks. Collect your things as fast as you can. There's no time." Only then did I realize that I was not being taken to the punishment cell, but rather was being transported somewhere. But why and where? I was told nothing.

A group of us were hurried out of the camp, accompanied by eight soldiers who were relaxed and casual. It was not until we were seated on a passenger train and tickets had been purchased that I began to grasp what was happening. In response to our questions, the officer in charge said, "I really don't know what all the rush and special treatment are for. All I can say is that at the end of the day we received orders to transfer you immediately to the prison in Perm. That's all I know."

We spent the night at the Perm prison. No one disturbed us until lunch time. Then the guards started summoning prisoners one at a time. I was second. Since the first prisoner had not returned, I didn't know where I was being taken or why. I did notice, though, that the guard was extremely polite. He didn't even tell me to put my arms behind my back. And he was a captain, not an ordinary soldier. We crossed through the courtyard and went up to an office on the second floor. He stopped at one door, knocked, and asked, "May we come in?"

"Come in," was the answer.

I hesitated in the corridor until the captain urged, "Please, come in." Then I saw a representative from the prosecutor's office, with two big stars on his shoulders. My file was open on the desk in front of him. After two trials in one term, it was pretty thick.

"You've probably noticed the changes taking place in our country lately," he began.

"Well, I've heard a little from the papers, but behind bars it's hard to know what's going on. You would know much better than I."

"Ah, yes!" he said with a smile. "I want to inform you that you have been pardoned from serving the rest of your term by the highest authorities, the Presidium of the Supreme Soviet. The order to release you is almost as good as in hand."

"What order?" I asked with great interest. "Have you actually received such an order?"

"Not exactly, but your case is very nearly decided. As far as the authorities are concerned, all this [he pointed to my file] is now in the past. But the government wants to know how you intend to act in the future, whether you'll continue to undermine authority and act in violation of Article 70."

I explained to him that I did not consider myself guilty of violating Article 70—that as a Christian, a church minister, I had no involvement in political activities. I had stated this during the investigation and the trial and had explained it at great length in my appeal.

"Could you please write out what you have just said?"

"Yes, I can," I answered, "but I've said all this before."

He gave me a sheet of paper, and I wrote at the top: "To the Presidium of the Supreme Soviet." He tried to help me word my statement as a request for a pardon, but I politely declined his help and said I could write it myself.

So I began, "I, Pyotr Vasilievich Rumachik, am not guilty of violating Article 70." I went on to say that I had already made this clear at my trial and that I had no intention of violating Article 70 in the future. I signed with the words, "Convicted on the basis of slanderous testimony by false witnesses, Pyotr Vasilievich Rumachik." The prosecutor's representative was not happy with my statement, but he took it anyway.

Then he asked me whether I wanted to stay in Perm or be taken back to the camp. "It's not my concern," I said. "It's your business where you hold me."

"Well, we'll send all this to Moscow, and it will be decided soon. But wouldn't you prefer to go back to camp? Or do you have enemies there?"

"None among the prisoners," I said, "but the administration has been making things very hard. In fact, I was expecting to be put in solitary confinement a few days ago." I told him what had happened during the past weeks, concluding, "All this happened just because I prayed openly. There were no violations of regime."

"Did you file a complaint?" he asked.

"I wrote one," I answered, "but then on the twentieth I was rushed out of the camp and had no chance to sign it."

"Well, I'll see to it that your statement is sent."

Back in the cell I found out that others were being called out and questioned in the same way. They had also been sentenced under Article 70. We waited together in this cell from January 21 until February 4.

Although the prosecutor had told me I was to be released, it was still hard to believe. I had been through so much, and had seen how devious those people can be. On our third or fourth day a doctor examined us all, and we started receiving good food. At first we thought it had been brought to us by mistake, and we refused it.

"Please take it," the guards insisted. "It's really for you." So we were fed well from then on.

On February 4 an officer came to the cell before lunch and said that on orders from the Supreme Soviet, we were all released as of February 2. "If we can get your documents and tickets taken care of today, then you can go. If not, then you'll leave tomorrow."

As it turned out, we left the next day. Once again, everything was rushed. The train station was a half hour's drive from the prison, and one hour before my train was scheduled to leave, I was given new clothing and told, "Quick, change as fast as you can! We've got to leave!" There wasn't even time for a search. They gave me some money and rushed me to the station. I boarded the train ten minutes before it was to leave. After the train had left the station I looked at my documents. They were stamped, "Pardoned." So I had received a pardon without asking for it!

As I sat there, traveling and thinking, I knew that soon I would be meeting my family and the church again. I

After his release from prison, Pastor Pyotr Rumachik is met at the train by his teenage daughter and other Christian friends.

Pastor Rumachik leads in this baby dedication service, a special time when parents promise before God and fellow Christians to train their children as Christians "in the fear and nurture of the Lord."

wondered what I could share with them. Even in the most dreary hours and when I had no strength at all, there was one basic thought that had never left me: the power of the prayers of God's people. Prayer is powerful and effective. The Lord hears prayers. When you pray, things happen. We see this throughout the Bible.

Today my heart is overwhelmed with gratitude to God, and with the psalmist I say, "Bless the LORD, O my soul, and forget not all his benefits" (Ps. 103:2). He never forsook me, not in my darkest, hardest hours. The promises of our Lord Jesus Christ work in all of life. When the Lord bid his disciples farewell on the Mount of Olives, he said to them—and through them to all Christians through the centuries—"Lo, I am with you alway, even unto the end of the world" (Matt. 28:20b). Sometimes we wonder if these words are true. But God has given this promise to each of us and wants us to know that he will never leave us, no matter what happens. For this reason, we should never stop praying. Our flesh may fail, our physical bodies may even die, but because we have God's promises, because we know God really hears us, we should always continue to pray fervently. God has always heard in the past; he still hears us today and will hear us tomorrow.

I would add that when God hears those who are suffering, he sends very special blessings. In spite of my circumstances, there were times in prison when I felt I was the happiest man on earth. Others said this to me, too: "You are the richest man of all!" I was rich because of the fellowship I had through letters. When I was returning to Chita from the Urals, I packed as many cards and letters as I could into a large bag and took them along. I had more than five hundred. The guards who searched me were always amazed.

"What's all this?" they would ask. "Where are you taking these?"

"These are mine. I have reasons for keeping them," I answered.

They looked through them, read some of them, and were surprised at what they read. Finally they shrugged their shoulders and said, "All right, take them and go!" Being able to keep the letters was a great blessing.

I am also thankful for the support I received in the form of petitions. In 1986, when I was allowed to look through the documents in the new case against me, I saw that they had a file of forty or fifty petitions on my behalf that had come in while the trial was in progress. My wife told me about many other petitions that are filed away somewhere in the official archives. Once when she went to see the prosecutor in Chita, during their conversation he threw a file down on the table and dozens of petitions spilled out. I was so encouraged to hear this. Brothers and sisters in Christ had put their shoulders next to mine and helped bear the burden of my bonds.

I am thankful, too, for those whose letters I never received. Many letters were withheld, and I do not know what those people wrote. But the Lord, in whose name they did it, knows what they wrote, where the letters ended up, and who prevented them from reaching me. Even though I never actually received them, they still lifted a cold cup of water to my lips, and such a deed is not unnoticed by the Lord. He will reward them.

The church has not traveled an easy road these last years. Some Christians, like me, were shackled in granite and iron, and others have endured all kinds of humiliations and persecutions and threats. The church has been under great pressure. But all this reminds me of a man laying asphalt on the ground. As he presses it down, the

Members of the Council of Evangelical Baptist Churches. Pastor Rumachik serves as vice president.

ground below undergoes a great load of pressure. Later, when you walk across that hard surface, you will often see a green shoot pushing up through the asphalt. That is the power of life! The church has endured great burdens, but the Spirit of God has penetrated the oppressive weight and given birth to new life. Many people have come to the Lord during the seven years I was absent. This is a manifestation of God's power. He has heard the prayers of the church and blessed her.

Our enemies counted on finishing off the church by persecuting us and putting us in bonds. They hoped at least to damage us beyond repair. But they were wrong. Just as the church survived and triumphed in previous centuries, so also in our day. The Lord will sustain the church by the power of his love until her mission on earth is complete. Then, with great rejoicing, she will go to meet her Lord.

The enemies cannot break the church by oppression, persecution, and threats, because the church is sustained by the living, active, and effective power of God's promises and the prayers that rise every day from earth to heaven. This is the work of our living Savior, who has authority over all. Praise God that the green shoots are strong and growing! May God grant that they may mature, blossom fragrantly, and bear fruit to the glory of our precious, living Lord.

5

Luba Skvortsova
Prison Graffiti

I often used to wonder, *What will happen to me if I get arrested?* Many of my friends were in prison. Galina Vilchinskaya, for example, a girl of my own age, was already serving her second term. In my prayers I asked the Lord, "Why must Galina walk this path again? If only I could serve her second term for her!" But, in his own timing, the Lord sent the testing that he had planned for me and led me down the path of bondage.

The first time I saw a prison from the inside, I was all eyes. As a guard led me through endless corridors, up

When Luba Skvortsova (b. 1959) went to a Christian friend's house in Gagry for a visit the evening of February 12, 1983, there was no warning that three long years would pass before she returned to her own home. Luba was arrested when police raided the premises. This happened just six days before her twenty-fourth birthday. Though not a member of the Council of Prisoners' Relatives, Luba assisted them whenever she could. She is now married.

stairs and around corners, I wondered if I could ever find my way out again. When we got all the way to the top floor, the guard locked me in a cell. I stood there holding my mattress and looked around. I noticed that even the small window was covered with an iron grill. Six women prisoners were looking me over carefully.

Finally one of them said, "What are you doing here, child?"

"I'm a Christian," I answered. "That's why I've been put here. But if I may, I'll tell you all about it tomorrow. Right now I only want to sleep. I was arrested two days ago. I was kept at the police station for questioning and have just been brought here."

The other prisoners agreed to let me rest and offered me a little soup left over from their dinner. I was glad to eat it.

I was in the same prison in Voroshilovgrad as some of our preachers who had been arrested: Pavel Rytikov, Stepan Germaniuk, Pavel Sazhnev, Ivan Tyagun, and Anatoly Balatsky. When these brothers in Christ found out that I was there, too, they wanted to encourage me somehow. One day as I was walking in the exercise yard, I saw these words hastily scribbled on one of the walls: "Be faithful unto death!" How encouraged I was to see this graffiti message, which was to give me much strength in the years that followed.

During my imprisonment I was very aware of the Lord's protection and could clearly see his answers to my prayers. In freedom many activities had distracted my attention. But in prison the Lord was always right beside me. In my thoughts I was constantly talking to him, and he provided immediately for every need. There was no one else to whom I could open my heart, so I took everything to the Lord in prayer, even simple decisions about how I should act.

Being in bonds was a blessing for me. I experienced joy there such as I had never known in freedom. The women in my cell would ask, "How can you be so calm and happy when you've been thrown in prison for nothing?" I rejoiced that I was suffering for the Lord's sake.

However, before my trial, I did experience feelings of alarm and uncertainty. I could not sleep the night before the trial but had spent the night in prayer, asking the Lord for wisdom and strength. The next morning, when the prison van pulled up to the court building, I saw my parents and many friends waiting outside. Although I wanted to weep for joy at seeing their faces after three months in prison, I controlled myself. I didn't want the persecutors to see my tears because they might say that I was crying because of doubts or fear. The Lord strengthened me and helped me not to cry.

The prison van stopped in front of the court building, but the guards didn't take me out. After a little while they told me the trial had been delayed, and they drove me back to the prison. After lunch I was taken back to the court building. This time the street was full of police, and they wouldn't let my friends even get near. Guards allowed my parents to come into the courtroom but seated them in the farthest corner. Papa immediately spoke up and said that he couldn't hear well, and he moved to the front to sit near me.

The trial lasted two days. For the reading of the verdict, all the Christians who had been waiting outside were allowed into the courtroom. When the judge read the sentence, three years of imprisonment, my friends started throwing flowers to me and shouting, "Take courage! Be faithful unto death!" They kept throwing flowers as I was taken back out to the van.

On the way to the camp, I prayed and asked the Lord

that I might find another Christian there. And the Lord answered! When I arrived at the camp, the other prisoners asked me what I had been sentenced for. After hearing my story, they said, "There's another believer here just like you!"

They introduced me to Maria Didnyak. It was so wonderful to meet her. Maria became like a mother to me. She protected me, helped me, and taught me how to act in the camp. The work was very hard, so from the first day I asked the Lord to help me meet my quotas. I believe that a Christian should always be an example, should always work well, because this is a very strong testimony to other people. I was afraid that I would not be able to do the work and meet my quotas, and this would be a bad example to the non-Christians. Every morning as my brigade was taken to work, I prayed about this. When I went to my section and sat at my work station, I kept praying, "Lord, bless my hands that I might be able to work quickly and well!" And even though the work was hard and we labored twelve hours a day, I was able to manage it.

During my first winter in the camp I got very sick and afterward had a hard time regaining my strength. When my parents came to visit me and saw the condition I was in, they were alarmed. They informed all our Christian friends about my condition and asked for prayer and petitions on my behalf. As a result I was given an easier work assignment and my health gradually improved.

Maria and I saw each other often. We would walk in the yard, sharing portions of Scripture, praying, and sometimes even singing very quietly. We talked about our friends, recited poems to each other, and had our own little worship services. Whenever either of us received a letter, we would read it together, rejoicing over every little piece of news. Several times the camp warden summoned us and told us not to meet anymore, but we could not live without this fellowship.

One time the guards searched our cots and night tables and found our little Gospel and a notebook with poems. They confiscated everything. We accepted this from the Lord. We prayed only that he would give us the strength to endure the punishment we would receive for possession of the Gospel. Shortly afterward we were summoned by the director of the camp. When we walked into her office, she looked at us and said, "I won't talk with you today! Tomorrow I'll gather all the camp administrators and you'll answer for your deeds before everyone!"

She seemed surprised that we remained so calm and conducted ourselves with Christian dignity. We walked back to our barracks and continued to pray about the situation.

The next day the whole administration gathered, and Maria and I were summoned. The head of the operative section announced that during a search Didnyak and Skvortsova were found to have a Gospel.

Everyone was interested. "Do you have this Gospel here?" they asked. "May we see it?"

The administrators passed it around, and they all looked at it very carefully. That moment was the first time many of them had ever seen a Gospel. Some of these people were highly educated, had graduated with law degrees, and had read much anti-religious literature, but they had never seen a Gospel! They began asking questions, and we had a very interesting conversation about God, the Bible, and our faith. No one even mentioned the search or our "violation" of possessing the Gospel. They seemed to have forgotten why they had summoned us and at the end didn't even tell us what our penalty would be for having the Gospel. Several days later Maria and I were told that we would be denied the privilege of having extra money to spend in the camp store. How we thanked the Lord for his protection and care, for we had expected solitary confinement!

When the day came for Maria to be released, I was both joyful and sad—happy that she would be at home with her family, could go to church meetings, and would see everyone, but sad that I would be left alone. My imprisonment had been brightened so much by the presence of my dear sister in Christ! But, then again, I had now gotten used to camp life. She had been there to help me during the hardest time, the early weeks of camp.

On the first day of our separation, I felt Maria's absence very keenly. There was no one I could share with and just talk to. But then the Lord became even closer. As I walked to and from work, I talked to the Lord all the time in my heart, and I thought, *How good it is to be with the Lord, so easy and free, even here in camp!* There are no words to describe what I experienced. The Lord is so close in such circumstances!

While I was in the camp, the Lord gave me many opportunities to help people, especially the elderly prisoners. One elderly lady broke her arm, so I took care of her and washed her clothes. And I liked to watch as the transports of new prisoners were brought into the camp. There was always hope in my heart that another Christian would be brought to the camp.

One day, as I was watching the new prisoners arrive, I spotted a woman who looked familiar. She looked like

Ulyana Germaniuk, the wife of one of our imprisoned pastors. I studied her face from a distance but decided it could not be her. This woman was too old and thin and gray. I knew Ulyana well and had seen her just before my arrest—she could not have changed so much in such a short time. Disappointed, I went back to my barracks.

A few days later someone said to me, "They brought another Baptist in on the new transport. Have you seen her yet?"

"Where is she?" I asked. "What barracks did they put her in?"

"She's sick. She's in the infirmary."

I ran to the infirmary and saw the same old lady I had noticed earlier. It *was* Ulyana! How she had changed! She could neither walk nor stand, and didn't even have the strength to talk. I began to spend every free moment with Ulyana, taking care of her. In two weeks she was discharged from the infirmary and sent to work. It was very hard for her. She could barely walk, much less work, so I continued taking care of Ulyana, washing her clothes and fixing her bed. As the day of my release approached, I could scarcely imagine what would happen to her after I left. On the day of our parting I went to say good-bye and we embraced. She asked me to give her greetings to all the friends who were praying for her and sent special greetings to the ladies of the Council of Prisoners' Relatives. Remembering them with love, she wanted to encourage them in their work. Ulyana also asked them to petition and pray for her, considering the poor condition of her health. She especially asked for petitions that she be relieved of her work in the camp, because she had absolutely no strength left.

As a prisoner, my favorite Bible verse was Revelation 2:10: "Fear none of those things which thou shalt suffer

Still wearing her prison uniform and jacket, Luba is welcomed home by her happy parents.

It was standing room only at the house church service where many friends gathered to welcome Luba home and to hear about her experiences in prison.

Both Luba and Andrei Yudintsev (*see* chap. 1) told of their arrests and prison years at this youth meeting.

. . . be thou faithful unto death, and I will give thee a crown of life." Many other verses from the Scriptures were also dear to me, but this one especially. For three years my main goal had been to remain faithful to the end.

Now, after my release, I sometimes wonder if this was only to be my first term. Anything can happen if we follow the Lord faithfully and walk the path on which he leads us without turning to the side. Even now, those words often resound in my heart: "Be faithful unto death!"

6

Veniamin Markevich
"Papa Captive"

Walking down the street in October 1982, I was on my way to visit a family in our church when a stranger suddenly called out.

"Veniamin Markevich, wait! We need you!"

I realized I was about to be arrested and quickened my pace. I was almost to my friends' home and wanted to reach it so they could let my family know where I was.

"No! Stop right there! Hold it!"

Two shouting men dashed across the street and stopped me. Next a police car pulled alongside and took

Veniamin Markevich (b. 1938) enjoyed freedom for just two short months before being imprisoned a second time in October 1982 at the age of 44. A member of the CEBC, Markevich is a pastor of the independent Baptist church in Ordzhonikidze and a gifted poet. Sentenced to five years, he was released eight months early in February 1987.

me away to prison. I was arrested, and nobody I knew had seen.

Sitting in the cell, thoughts of unfinished plans whirled through my mind. On that day I had planned to visit several Christian families and to preach at the prayer meeting. For the next day my wife and I had planned to drive to a neighboring city to see our relatives. (I had been freed from my first prison term just two months earlier and still had not visited them). For the end of the week, I had looked forward to attending a conference of fellow ministers. Suddenly all my hopes and plans had been dashed—I was under arrest.

I had not expected to be arrested so soon after my release, and the realization that no one knew weighed heavily on my heart. Three days, later, however, the guards handed me some food and warm clothing from my wife. These gifts reassured me—at least my family knew where I was.

Later I learned that the authorities had arrested three ministers from our church: Veniamin Chistyakov, Vasily Mikhin, and me. By the end of December, the investigator let us prepare for the trial. Four days in a row, we were led to an office where we could examine the testimonies of the witnesses and other materials in the investigator's presence.

The third of these days was December 25, Christmas Day. That morning, as soon as we entered the office, Veniamin Chistyakov turned to the investigator. "Today is Christmas," he said. "All Christians celebrate this day. Let us pray together."

The investigator agreed. We three then quietly sang "Silent Night" and knelt, giving the Lord thanks in prayer for the birth of his Son on earth. The investigator sat and listened in silence. As soon as we finished praying but while we were still on our knees, the door opened, and a KGB worker stepped into the office. He saw what was happening, quickly stepped back into the corridor, and closed the door behind him. He did not come back the rest of the day.

My wife told me later that she had seen the investigator early on Christmas morning. When he was riding the bus to work, my wife and our two younger children were riding the same bus to the holiday morning worship service (the older children were in school, since Christmas is usually a working day in our country). She greeted the investigator, wished him a Merry Christmas, and asked him to pass Christmas greetings to Papa from the children.

Our trial lasted from January 24 to February 2. On the first day, when the police car drove up to the building of the trial, Veniamin, Vasily, and I saw about a hundred and fifty Christian friends on the snow-covered square! Many had requested leave from work so they could be there to cheer and support us.

During the trial, even some of the testimonies against us were encouraging. One teacher declared, "Our school has a great atheistic program, but because of the activities of the defendants, practically nothing comes of it!"

The testimonies of the believers also cheered us up. One young Christian woman said, "I can't testify against my brothers in Christ. May the Lord help me!"

Then, answering a question from the judge about the criminal actions of the defendants, a young man stated, "These are my brothers! I know them to be honorable citizens, good husbands and fathers. They haven't committed any crime. Their only 'fault' is in being Christians. But I'm also a Christian, and I'm ready to sit on the defendants' bench with them if being a Christian is a crime in our country."

In the end the court convicted us: Vasily Mikhin to three years, Veniamin Chistyakov to four years, and me to five years' deprivation of freedom.

My transport from the Caucasus to Yakutia in Siberia lasted a hundred days and took me through many prisons. At the prison in Solikamsk, I spent many days pondering the seventeenth chapter of the Gospel of John, which I knew by heart. This chapter is the high-priestly prayer of Jesus before his death on the cross. In the prayer the Lord mentions "glory" six times. For example, he asks the Father to glorify his Son, and he testifies that he himself glorified his Father by his earthly life, completing the work ordained by the Father. I especially considered what Jesus said about his followers: "And the glory which thou gavest me I have given them . . ." (John 17:22).

How does God produce his eternal glory? I wondered. *And if before the sufferings on the cross Jesus Christ spoke so much about the eternal glory of God, this must be something important and meaningful.* Prison life suddenly became easy and joyous as I concentrated on the glory of God.

Something unexpected also happened in Solikamsk: the guards summoned me for a visit! *With whom?* I wondered. In this faraway Ural city—over six hundred miles from home—who could come to visit me? The guards led me to the visiting room, and there was my wife!

We were permitted a thirty-minute meeting, but even such a short meeting was a precious gift. My wife told

Mrs. Markevich took four sons to visit their father at the prison camp near Yakutsk, Siberia. The Markevichs have eleven children.

me that our oldest daughter was now engaged to the son of my friend Veniamin Chistyakov, who had been tried with me. I passed along my approval and blessings and promised to pray for them. I thanked my heavenly Father for his concern for my children, for their needs, and—most importantly—for their souls.

When I was arrested the first time, this daughter who was going to get married was thirteen years old. My wife's sister had come to our house to visit and started spouting a lot of nonsense: "What kind of husband do you have? What's he thinking? Here he is in prison, and you're alone with the children! And not just two or three children, but a houseful! Is this how he takes care of his family?"

After she left, my thirteen-year-old daughter asked, "Why didn't you answer Aunt like Jesus did to Peter: 'You do not have in mind the things of God, but the things of men'?" Now this little daughter was an adult and going to marry a young preacher!

As soon as I got back to the cell after my wife's visit, I started to write wedding congratulations and my wishes for my daughter and her future husband. I prayed that the censor would not delay this letter and that the Lord would help them to receive it. They did get the letter in time, and the exhortations from the papa/prisoner were so special to the bride and groom that my letter was read to everyone at the wedding celebration.

On my way across the country, I met many prisoners who had been in a camp or prison with Christians. One prisoner gave me the address of Nikolai Boiko and told me about him. In another prison I met a man who proudly announced that in camp he had eaten at the same table with Boiko for many months. He recounted how Boiko received everything with a smile, even though the guards often put him in isolation. I was encouraged to hear such testimonies.

At last I arrived in the camp in Yakutia in July 1983. I ended up getting along well with the other prisoners. Many asked what I was in for and why I had been sent so far from home. I told them about the Lord.

Rudolph Klassen had been at that camp right before me. An elderly Yakut told me, "Once I was put in isolation for some offense, and Rudolph was already there for telling people about Christ. He was so bold! The administration had already extended his term once, but all the same he didn't betray the Lord. He told me much about God there."

Many prisoners at that camp still remember Georgi Vins. Some would say, "Do you know Vins? He was imprisoned with us here for four years. I often drank tea with him," or "We worked together." All of these were good testimonies.

On a neighboring bunk slept one prisoner, a thief who had already served six terms. He fell sick and I took care of him. When we got better acquainted, I started to tell him about Christ. I even gave him my little Gospel of John.

"You know, Veniamin," he confided to me, "as soon as you settled into our barracks, you made an impression on me. I noticed you're not like the others."

But as soon as administration representatives saw me having conversations with him, they summoned him for interrogation, threatened that he had better tell what we talk about.

"I didn't know you were being shadowed here!" he later said to me. "I didn't tell them what you told me about God. I didn't want you to get punished for it." So we started being more cautious. We didn't talk in the barracks but met somewhere outside. This man became fond of the Gospel and often read it secretly.

Then winter arrived—my first northern winter. In Yakutia snow starts to fall in early September and never melts until June. It gets deep. Even when the temperature dropped to −76° Fahrenheit, my construction brigade kept working in the open air. However, the Lord wondrously helped me to bear the cold.

In 1984 another preacher was brought to the camp—Nikolai Popov from Ryazan. How I rejoiced on the arrival of a brother in Christ! How I thanked the Lord! Every day we met outside to pray, share news from home, and sometimes read through a few verses from the Gospel.

Nikolai and I celebrated Christmas together that year.

Veniamin Markevich looks at some of the letters he received while in prison.
What's the best way to encourage a prisoner? Letters, letters, letters.

December was bitterly cold, and the snow stood high. In the barracks area pits for something had just been dug, and bonfires were burning there to thaw out the ground a little. Nikolai and I met at one of these bonfires, quietly sang "Silent Night," and prayed together. We exchanged greeting cards and letters from our families and friends.

The letters we received were excellent. Sometimes they included whole chapters from the Bible. One time, however, the brigade leader didn't give me one of my letters right away. Instead he summoned me for a discussion about it.

"It appears the girl who wrote this letter is still very

young," he said. "But here she writes you such lines from a poem: 'To be a Christian—that means repaying evil with good.' What good words! And she signs 'Your sister.' Is it by blood relationship?"

"Yes," I answered, "by the blood of Christ!"

"Hm, I thought as much." And he gave me the letter.

The letters from my own children were an exceptional blessing. Once I received a letter from the youngest, my eleventh little child. He had not yet started school but printed these words in pencil: "Papa, I'm waiting for you! Tell the guards to let you go home." His letter was so touching. After all, my youngest son barely remembered me; he was still pretty tiny when I was arrested. Later I heard that he had learned the children's song "When the Lanterns Are Lit and All the Papas Go Home After Work" and often sang it. One evening he said, "Mama, the lanterns are already lit, so why doesn't Papa come home? Don't they light lanterns in Siberia?"

One time, though, an officer summoned me and said, "A greeting card for you came from your daughter, and she calls you 'Papa captive.' What is all this? We don't have captives in this country, just prisoners. If she writes this again, I'll send her card to the police in your home town, and they'll let her know just what a captive is!"

I answered, "*Captive* is a biblical term. . . ."

"The Bible isn't recognized here!" he stormed. "Write her and tell her."

I wrote to my daughter, describing this conversation with the officer, and at Easter she wrote on a postcard, "Dear Papa, imprisoned for the Word of God: holiday greetings! Christ arose!" My family supported me, both my wife and children, and for me this encouragement was precious.

Eventually I was transferred to a different camp. On

my first day there an officer summoned me and warned me not to tell a single person about God. "If you start to preach here, I'll beat you." he said. "And nobody will punish me for it. I'll be in the right! There is no God; and even if he did exist, I'd shoot him!"

I had never heard such terrible words said about God, but I didn't answer. I walked back to the barracks and started to pray for the Lord to help me in this situation. And the Lord heard me: before long this officer was transferred to another camp.

I often sang. I recalled the words of David: "Thy statutes have been my songs in the house of my pilgrimage" (Ps. 119:54). However, my main comfort and encouragement came from the Bible chapters I had memorized. These verses gave food to my soul and helped in the struggle against the demonic powers that the apostle Paul writes about in Ephesians 6:11–12. Those were just such "evil days" when special strength was needed in order "having done all, to stand" (v. 13). The Lord gave victory through prayer, through the Word of God, and through his mighty name. Victory in sufferings for the Lord is possible only through the power of God.

But even though I had inner peace, I often wondered, *Why have so few people turned to the Lord through my witnessing? Why has there been no mass salvation of souls?* I testified of Christ as often as possible but saw little visible results.

The soil of these prisoners' hearts was, as the parable of the sower describes, ". . . by the way side" (Matt. 13:4). Because human hearts are so saturated with atheism and deep moral depravity, the seed of the Word of God, when planted in such hearts, gets snatched away. Many people questioned me about God out of curiosity, but only isolated individuals sincerely desired to learn about the Lord and to obey his Word.

For example, you may spend a lot of time talking with one person and telling him about God, and he shows great interest. With other people you establish good relations, but as soon as you touch upon faith in God, they refuse to discuss the subject.

When you talk to a third kind of person, he simply sticks to his own opinions. I had such an experience. After a conversation about God, one prisoner told me, "There's no difference between us. You're a believer, and I'm a believer. You pray, and I pray, too!" But when I brought up obedience to the Bible, he replied, "I never read the Bible, and I don't want to. I don't believe what's written in it." Then he didn't want to talk anymore.

Sometimes I wished I could take the megaphone the officers used to give orders and at least once give a sermon on salvation and repentance to everyone at once! Of course, that never happened; it just remained a dream.

In the end I concluded that the Lord sends Christians into bonds for one purpose: to tell sinners they will perish if they do not find salvation in Christ. As God's Word tells us, "When I say unto the wicked, Thou shalt surely die; and thou givest him not warning, nor speakest to warn the wicked from his wicked way, to save his life; the same wicked man shall die in his iniquity; but his blood will I require at thine hand" (Ezek. 3:18).

7

Mikhail Azarov
The Newspaper Saint

Here, take this for Kryuchkov!" one of the men shouted, punching me.

I had just come from a meeting at my factory, where KGB agents told slanderous lies about Christians and reviled the Evangelical Baptist Churches. As a result, people were so enraged against believers that several of them jumped me right there on the street.

"And take that for Vins!"

Other people on the street, however, began pulling my attackers off me, and I managed to escape alive.

Soon after this beating, the authorities searched the

Mikhail Azarov (b. 1935) was arrested in August 1984 because of his ministry as pastor of the independent Baptist church in Belgorod. He was sentenced to five years in Soviet labor camps, his second term for the gospel's sake. He was then 48 years old. Pastor Azarov was freed unexpectedly in March 1987. He and his wife, Nadia, are the parents of five children.

homes of many believers, including mine. The public
prosecutor later told me that they were expecting to find
money, but of course they did not: we had none. They
did, however, find two Christian magazines in my home.
I was arrested and charged on the basis of Articles 190
and 227 of the Criminal Code. Article 190 concerns
"slander against Soviet reality." Article 227 deals with
leading young people astray, distributing literature, and
several other activities. Violation of Article 227 carries a
punishment of five years' imprisonment.

I spent four months in prison before being brought to
court. I was locked up with about ten prisoners who were
mostly high-ranking people, such as engineers and direc-
tors. They all felt sure I had been arrested by mistake.
They could hardly believe that in our country a person
can be arrested just for his beliefs. Many of them assured
me that the authorities would apologize for this mistake
and let me go home. Several even gave me their addresses
so I could go to their homes and tell their wives where
they were. None of them expected me to be sentenced to
a long term.

In prison I always told people openly that I was arrested because I am a Christian. I also prayed openly and
talked a lot about God. Most prisoners were willing to
agree that God exists, but it seemed they only wanted to
use him. For example, they wondered if he could help
them get a shorter sentence.

I sang in the cell, especially in the evenings. The others enjoyed listening. Several times the guards warned
me that singing was prohibited, but I continued to do it
anyway.

At Christmas time I made a sign: "For unto you is
born this day a Savior, which is Christ the Lord." I had
only one piece of paper, but I managed to fit all the words

on it in pretty big letters. One of my cellmates, a chief engineer, helped me. A guard saw it.

"That's a good sign," he said. "But why didn't you include the date of his birth?"

So I did.

Shortly before New Year a KGB colonel and two majors came to see how I was getting along. "Did you know two of your friends have gone to God?" they asked.

Of course, I had heard nothing about it.

"Do you know Boris Artiushenko?"

"Yes, he's my friend," I said.

"Well, he's dead," said the colonel. "He didn't want to go on living, so he's gone to God."

Boris and I had been arrested at about the same time. Apparently he died in prison. The other man was Yefim, a preacher from my church who had opened his house for worship services. What could I do when I heard about the deaths of these two close friends? I prayed to God and committed into his hand all that yet lay ahead of me.

"Don't you want to be where they are? We can help you," the colonel threatened as he signaled the end of the interrogation.

At last I was taken to court. The trial lasted three days. During that time I fasted, as did many of my Christian friends. I asked God for only one thing—to help me remain faithful to him.

Many people came to the trial: public officials, atheists, television and radio reporters, and many Christians. The judge, who was an elderly man, said he had never seen so many people in a courtroom at once. On the third day my sentence was read: five years' deprivation of freedom in labor camp.

Before long I was loaded onto a prison car for transport. One of the prisoners on the train eyed me carefully for a minute and then shouted, "Hey, fellows, this is the saint we read about in the paper, the one who said at his trial that he prays for prisoners!"

At my trial the judge had asked whether I admitted some connection with Christian prisoners. "Of course," I said. "They're my brothers, and I pray for them." All of this was printed in the newspapers. The judge had been referring to believers, but the men on the train took it to mean that I pray for all prisoners. The newspaper article helped me greatly. The atheists had intended it for evil, but the article served me well and opened many doors.

When this man announced that a saint was on the train, another prisoner pushed his way over, fell on his knees in front of me, and began to sob. He asked me to put my hands on his head and pray for mercy for him. He had seen them pray that way in the Orthodox Church and wanted me to absolve him of his sins.

His situation was desperate. He had killed several people and was now on his way to camp to pay for his crime. We talked all the way to Voronezh, and I explained the Gospel to him. Other prisoners were listening, too, and occasionally said, "Speak up—we can't hear." When we reached the prison, the man and I were separated.

I was taken to my cell, and it turned out that a newspaper from my home district had preceded me. The prisoners already knew who I was. Right away they began questioning me about my faith.

"My grandfather is a believer, and I'm going to do everything I can to help you," announced one young man. He stayed close to me and even tried to give me his food. From what he said and did, it was clear his grandfather was a good Christian.

I was in the Voronezh prison for about a month. We were extremely overcrowded, with very little air to breathe and nowhere to lie down. Prisoners were huddled up even under the bunks.

From Voronezh I was taken to the prison in Chelyabinsk, where I spent twenty-eight days and encountered the most horrible experience of my years in prison. Whenever anyone was transferred to Chelyabinsk from another prison, the prisoners asked him, "Do they do 'no limits' there?" "No limits" refers to the ruthless conduct of a criminal gang who terrorize other prisoners and do whatever comes into their heads.

Yura was the leader of just such a criminal band in our cell. He was young and strong, built like a giant. His father, mother, and three brothers were all in prison, and Yura himself was in for the second time. In the evening one of the gang would watch for the guards and Yura would give the order: "I want to see blood!" They did terrible things to the other prisoners, some of which are too shameful to speak of.

They never touched me, but the shrieks and groans of the other men were heartrending. Double doors separated us from the guards, so they never heard what was going on. And Yura's gang kept an eye out, because they would be punished if they were caught.

After fifteen days in this cell, I could bear the savagery no longer. "Lord," I prayed, "this is beyond my strength." Suddenly a Bible verse came to mind: "I give unto you power to tread . . . over all the power of the enemy . . ." (Luke 10:19). I felt that the Lord was directing me to take the offensive, but I really didn't know what might happen.

That evening, when Yura began to give the orders, I walked over, took hold of his arm and said, "Yura, the Scriptures say don't do to others what you don't want them to do to you."

Everyone watched to see what would happen. Those who were beaten and wounded looked at me with hope that maybe the evening would pass quietly, without violence.

Yura pulled his arm away. "I don't want to hurt you, old man. But when the wild beast in me is aroused, you'd better watch out. Go sit on your bunk."

"Listen, Yura," I said, "let's make a deal. You give me just one hour to talk, and I'll tell you about my past."

"Well, you always tell the truth. I know that much. And it's true we don't know anything about you." He turned to his comrades. "Should we let him talk?" They shrugged. "All right," said Yura. "Start talking."

So I told them about Christians and how we are persecuted. I talked about the arrests and fines, the disruption of worship services. I talked for an hour, then two, then three. By then it was time for lights out.

"This has been interesting," Yura said, "but the evening's gone. You told me that Christ said not to do to others what you don't want done to yourself. I want to hear more." The guards had entered the hall, and the prisoners had to get into their bunks, so I promised to continue the next evening.

Two prisoners hardly let me sleep that night. They kept sneaking to my bunk and questioning me, demanding that I defend my faith. They were both well educated, about forty, and had endured such humiliations at the hands of Yura and his gang that blood still oozed from their wounds.

For the next ten evenings it was the same. The prisoners would come to me and say, "Please talk about Jesus. We will gladly listen. Just do something to stop this madness!"

So I continued speaking on the theme "Don't do to

others what you don't want done to yourself." It was difficult, of course, to keep Yura from crying for more blood. But somehow I was allowed to talk, and the prisoners listened and asked all kinds of questions. Other prisoners started asking to be put in my cell. They wanted protection. The warden, though, saw things differently. He was afraid I would influence them to become believers.

After Chelyabinsk we passed through two other prisons before we came to Krasnoyarsk. In all, I spent over two months in five different prisons. Toward the end of March I finally arrived at the camp in Nishny Ingash near Krasnoyarsk. This camp was pretty bad, and even the warden admitted it was overcrowded. In the barracks the bunks were stacked in tiers of three. There was no way to get rid of the lice because we never had enough water to wash. What little water we had was brought in on trucks. Men were dying of hunger and cold.

I found out that another Baptist, Aleksei Kalyashin (*see* chapter 12), had been there before me. The men in the barracks remembered him well and even pointed out the bunk where he had slept. They showed me some greeting cards he had received and had left with them. I rejoiced to read the Scripture verses on the cards because I had no Bible there. Apparently Aleksei did have some Scripture with him. He was now gone but had left a good testimony, and the men who knew him treated me well.

I was poorly dressed because most of my belongings had been stolen, and the temperature dropped to $-22°$ Fahrenheit. But the other prisoners found me a hat and some socks, which were a great treasure even though they were torn. I was thankful for all they shared. The camp director did not treat me badly, but his superiors imposed harsh restrictions on me. They said I would be severely punished if I talked to anyone about God.

In the camp one is always cold and hungry, which is a great hardship. On top of this, my first work assignment was torturous. I had to carry lumber at a sawmill. Because I had back problems, carrying heavy loads caused me acute pain. I was sent to the infirmary, where they examined me and acknowledged that I really did have back problems, so I was transferred to lighter work.

Before six months had passed, the guards found some greeting cards I had received in the possession of other prisoners. They accused me of distributing them and put me in isolation for two months. After that, in October 1986, I was moved to the punishment cell for six months. I was denied all privileges, use of the camp commissary, and visits with my family. The warden called me to his office and told me I was an enemy of the people and of my country. He told the head of the punishment block to starve me and said he himself would shoot me at the first opportunity. Then I was sent back into isolation.

But, in the midst of these trials, God gave me strength to pray and not despair. God knows our path and our desires. While I was locked in the isolation cell, my legs became badly swollen, and I developed a serious rash. The difficulties were so great that I even prayed, "Lord, it's too much for me. Take my soul." About this time, the warden came by my cell to see how I was doing. He saw I was in bad shape and ordered the guards to unlock the bed from the wall and fold it down so I could lie down during the daytime. I was also given some lotion for the rash. The Lord helped me. The swelling in my legs went down, and the crisis passed.

The KGB often came to talk with me. They mocked

and threatened and said, "You'll be here until you change
your beliefs. We'll just keep extending your sentence until you give in."

I didn't doubt their ability to carry out their threats,
but I kept hoping in God because I knew the mercy and
the power of the Lord. While I was in the punishment
block, KGB agents from Belgorod traveled to the camp to
talk to me but wouldn't give their names. One of them
came four or five times. He showed me his identification
from a distance, but I couldn't read his name. He questioned me on many subjects. He also accused our brotherhood and the Council of Evangelical Baptist Churches
of betraying our country. He demanded that we quit publishing Christian literature, that we stop petitioning, and
that we cooperate with the KGB. I always answered him
straightforwardly and refused to collaborate in any way.
After such conversations I was not given any medical
attention for a long time.

Because the KGB was familiar with the work of the
Council of Prisoners' Relatives, I was warned that if
people outside the camp found out about my situation,
new charges would be brought against me and my wife.
They didn't want God's people to know what was happening to me. But I managed to get word to my wife
about everything being taken away from me and my
weak physical condition.

When God's children wrote petitions on my behalf, it
showed they had not forgotten me. The authorities objected, of course, and told me to write my friends and tell
them to stop petitioning. Yet, whenever telegrams and
petitions came to the camp, my situation always improved. I was very grateful to the Lord and to my friends
for this help.

I was always glad to get letters. For a prisoner it means

a lot to receive mail. When you read a letter, you forget for a while that you are in bonds. You just rejoice and thank God. On December 25 I heard a guard coming down the corridor announcing, "Glory to God in the highest, and on earth peace, good will toward men." I was surprised, of course. He announced it again and then walked over to the door of my cell in the punishment block and asked, "Mikhail Azarov, you wouldn't happen to know who receives letters that say such things?"

"*I* do," I admitted.

He handed me a big bundle of letters, about a hundred and fifty from all corners of the country. I read them and re-read them and thanked God. I also received letters and cards from abroad. I was touched by people's concern, especially to know we have friends in other countries who support us in their prayers.

In the punishment cell I was put with the worst prisoners, people the ordinary criminals didn't want to be around. But God helped me to persuade them to stop their terrible sin and violence, and they generally treated me well.

During my fifth month in the punishment block, several other prisoners and I were moved to a very cold cell. Then they were moved out. Other prisoners were moved in and out of that cell, but I was always left there. I cannot describe how cold it was. My joints became so swollen that I was unable to bend my elbows or knees. I felt frozen to the core. All I could do was hope in God. Several times I asked the guards to move me out, but they always mocked, "If you need anything, pray to your God."

Before my release an official about thirty-five years old started coming to the camp to talk to me. He never told me his last name; he just said he had been commissioned by the Soviet government to talk to me because the authorities were reviewing all cases of believers. He came four or five times and tried to persuade me to write a document saying I was guilty as charged—that I had been engaged in distributing anti-Soviet slander, and that the Council of Prisoners' Relatives publishes slander against Soviet reality. What could I say? Of course I disagreed with every point and refused to write or sign any such document. Then the official told me the government was not opposed to releasing me, but I must sign just one document saying I was willing to collaborate with the KGB. I answered that as a Christian I could not sign such a paper. Despite my weakened physical condition, I knew I could not sign.

The last time the man came to see me, he said, "There's a plane leaving today and you can be on it—but you must sign this quickly, or you'll miss it." He handed me a document that said I acknowledged myself to be guilty and asked for mercy.

"I can't sign this," I said. "If there's an order to release me, of course I want to leave. But I haven't changed my views about registration, military service, the CEBC, the Council of Prisoners' Relatives, the Christian Publishing House, or our brotherhood. I consider everything to be right and in its proper place."

Finally he sighed, "Just write whatever you want."

So I wrote that I, Mikhail Azarov, sentenced for alleged violation of certain articles of the Criminal Code, was not guilty of anti-Soviet activity, that if the Soviet government was reviewing religious cases, they should review mine as well, and that if they wanted to release me, I would like to be sent home.

The official did not want to accept my statement, but he finally took it and left. About two weeks passed, and

Mikhail Azarov receives a Bible as a welcome home gift.

Preaching at an outdoor worship service in the spring of 1988.

my physical condition deteriorated rapidly. I was constantly chilled to the bone, I had severe heart pains, and I couldn't sleep at night. On Sunday, March 22, I spent the whole night in prayer. I was freezing. I felt I couldn't go on any longer, and I bid farewell to life. The next day, March 23, at four o'clock in the afternoon, a guard opened the door of my cell and called, "Mikhail Azarov, congratulations! I have good news for you. We've received orders for your release."

I could not believe it! Not long before, I had been told that the administration was planning to give me six more months in the punishment block, and that I would never get out. They had deprived me of visits and food parcels and, seeing the shape I was in, thought that I wouldn't survive till the end of my term. But the Lord had other plans for me. Now I was free.

On March 24 I was summoned to the warden's office. "Mikhail Azarov," the warden said, "I congratulate you with all my heart. The Soviet government has decided to release you early. I'm very happy for you. So be careful. Don't come back here. Even though you're our enemy, I feel sure you're changing your mind." He ordered the guards to give me shoes, clothing, and some money that my wife had sent for me.

I had to walk to the train station two miles away, and I was barely able to move. But the Lord did not abandon me. A car pulled up and the driver offered me a ride. He stopped at a little store where I bought some bread and candy. I was so hungry, it seemed I would never get enough bread. Then he took me to the train station in town. I bought a hat, scarf, and gloves, and took the next train.

When I arrived in Krasnoyarsk around eleven at night, I went to the apartment of an old friend who didn't recognize me until I took off my hat and scarf. Suddenly he realized that a former prisoner was standing before him. He threw his arms around me and wept. The first thing I wanted to do was get warm.

I stayed there for a few days and saw other Christians. My friend took good care of me, and I began to gain strength. Then I flew to Moscow, where my wife and two sons met me. At last I returned to Belgorod, my home town. Many friends had gathered at my house to greet me. I was so thin that some people didn't even recognize me. They gave me a wonderful homecoming—so many friends, so many flowers! Many were crying, and so was I.

At the worship service that evening I talked about my experiences. Everyone was amazed that I survived. But I think it is better to have a sick body and a healthy soul rather than the opposite.

The Lord had kept me. What a joy to believe in God, to depend on him, and to know that he is our Defender. The Lord gave me grace to keep hoping in him and trusting him through those dark days. As Christ said, ". . . If they have persecuted me, they will also persecute you . . ." (John 15:20). May he help us all.

8

Mikhail Khorev
Out of the Afrikanka

[*From his son*] *Early in the morning on December 19, 1986, our family was getting ready to go to the prison gate to meet our father, who was due for release that day. But at seven o'clock the doorbell rang. Mother opened the door, and there stood Papa in his prison uniform. We all hugged him and greeted him. As it turned out, a large crowd of our Christian friends had already gathered at the prison—children, teenagers, and adults from Moldavia and many cities all over the country. The authorities didn't want a large crowd to greet Papa at the very entrance to the prison, so they put him in a car and*

Mikhail Khorev (b. 1931) is known among believers in Russia as a fiery evangelist and dedicated youth worker. His steadfast adherence to Scripture and his warm, gentle humor make him a favorite among old and young alike. Soviet authorities are also interested in Pastor Khorev's ministry (CEBC) and have imprisoned him a total of twelve and a half years because of it. His most recent term ended in December 1986. He and his wife, Vera, have three sons.

*secretly drove him home. So there he was. Before we
even had a chance to pray, those who had been waiting
at the prison began to arrive. Soon the place was over-
flowing with people and flowers. Then Papa preached his
first sermon in seven years, based on Acts 12:*

King Herod raised his hand against some of the
apostles, and the authorities arrested Peter and James.
These were no ordinary arrests, because these men were
apostles, pillars in the church. What fear must have filled
the hearts of those early Christians: "What will happen
to us if all our leaders are arrested?"

In our country this year marks the twenty-fifth anniversary of our CEBC brotherhood, so we already have
twenty-five years of experience walking on this thorny
path. Actually, when we consider the whole history of
the church, we have almost two thousand years of experience. Even so, when all our leaders are arrested, we are
suddenly anxious and wonder what will happen to us
next. How much more that small handful of believers in
Jerusalem must have trembled when their leaders were
arrested. After all, we have the Book of Acts. We can have
hope and have confidence on the basis of what's written
in the New Testament. Those early Christians, though,
didn't have that. And suddenly Herod raised his hand
against some of the leaders of the church.

But now notice that Herod raised his hand against
some of the leaders of the church but not all. Why did he
not have them all arrested? After all, there were not that
many Christians. He could have taken them all and put
an end to the church. Did he lack determination? Was he
lacking in evil intentions? I think he had enough of both.
So why did he take only some of them?

The situation in their day was the same as it is in ours.

Still in his prison uniform, Mikhail Khorev takes time out for a family photograph the day he was released from prison.

The authorities can do only what God allows. Any action they take is controlled from above, and they must have a sanction from God. Just as you cannot be put in prison without a sanction from the prosecutor, in the same way the authorities cannot raise their hands against Christians without a sanction from God.

Herod raised his hand against several leaders of the church. James was arrested, and you know what happened to him—he was beheaded, because this was sanctioned by God. Peter was also arrested, but his case turned out quite differently. The prison gates were opened, and Peter walked out, because God is the One who sets the limits and determines what the enemy may and may not do.

Do you know how I felt when the gates opened for me today? The guards rushed me out of my cell and into a car and sped off. I said, "Where are you going in such a hurry?" As it turned out, you were all there waiting for me at the prison. They had to get me out of there fast! And when I was released today, I felt it was a greater miracle than when Peter was released. Why? Because when Peter left the prison, the guards were all asleep, but in my case, they were wide awake, and they put me out with their eyes open. And I say, "Lord, is there anything too hard for you? Are there any limits to your power?"

So let's not be discouraged when we hear that some of God's people are in difficult circumstances or that a brother or sister has been imprisoned. All of this is sanctioned by God, and the enemy cannot hold us for an extra minute if the sanction runs out.

I thank God for the divine sanctions that have been over the church for two thousand years. I thank the Lord for the faithfulness of men and women against whom Herod raised his hand, who experienced bonds. I thank him, too, for those who were not arrested but who were ready to accept anything they encountered on the path by which God led them.

While I was in the prison camps, I always prayed, "Lord, you see the men around me. When can I speak to them about you?" They were rough, some so degenerate they no longer seemed human. I would say, "Lord, your servant is ready to talk about you. You give me the opportunity and prepare the soil." Sometimes weeks or months would pass and I would not be able to talk to anyone. So what could I do? I simply lived before them as a Christian. At other times, however, I was able to talk to people every day and sometimes see immediate fruit from the conversation.

For example, one time in the camp in Omsk I had been locked in isolation for fifteen days and was required to check in at the office before returning to the main camp. About fifteen officers were there when I went in. I told the warden I had just come from isolation and requested permission to return to the main camp. He told me to go ahead but warned me to watch out.

"Listen, Khorev," said one of the officers, "I have a question for you. Do you really believe in God, or is this some kind of game?"

Thank you, Lord, I prayed silently. *This is just what I asked for.*

"Why do you want to know?" I answered.

"Well, maybe you get something out of it. Or maybe it's some quirk of yours. How should I know?"

"The answer is yes. I do believe in God."

"I don't believe you really believe in God."

"Look," I said, "there are fifteen of you here, and I don't believe you are all unbelievers, that not even one of you secretly prays to God."

"Watch it, Khorev!" the warden interrupted. "I can bring another criminal case against you right now for those words! That's religious agitation. According to our constitution, I have a right to engage in anti-religious agitation, but religious agitation is prohibited by Article 142 of the Criminal Code. You can get three more years for violating the *1929 Legislation on Religious Cults.* Go back to the barracks and write a report of what you said here, and we'll file a new case against you."

"I'm ready to serve three more years," I told him. "If just one of the fifteen of you becomes a Christian, it will be worth it."

I left and returned to my barracks. For some reason, though, nothing came of it. The warden didn't call me back. Afterward, I ran into several of those officers individually. All of them greeted me courteously. One told me that although his parents were Christians, he had never told anyone before. He said he had always prayed to God, ever since he was a child.

On another occasion, when all the prisoners were going into a building to check in with the guards, an officer across the yard yelled to me something about my boots not being clean and called me into his office. As it turned out, he was just looking for a way to talk to me alone. For years he had been tortured by doubts about whether God exists, and he wanted to speak to me. During the rest of my time at the camp, he did things from time to time to help me. So the Lord gave me fruit from that one little incident.

During my years in bonds, I met prisoners from all corners of the country. One man told me this story when he found out I am a Christian:

"We were on a prison transport heading east toward Khabarovsk," he said. "There was only one girl in our train, and she was a Christian. I never learned her name. That girl sang throughout the journey, day after day. For some reason, the guards didn't stop her. She just kept singing.

"Usually prisoners are crude when they see a woman. They mock and laugh and say all kinds of vulgar things. But nobody said anything bad to this girl. Her singing affected all of us. 'Sing some more!' 'Write down the words for me!' the men called out to her. Some said to the guard, 'Sergeant, tell her to keep singing. Walk her through the car so we can see her face.'

"And when she sang, a hush fell over our train car. Even the most hardened criminals, men who had served several terms, turned their heads to hide their tears."

"What did she sing?" I asked. "What were the words of her songs?"

"I don't remember the words," he answered, "but I can still feel her songs in my heart."

I offered to sing a few hymns to see if he recognized any that the girl had sung. I sang one, then another, then a third. Each time he said, "No, that wasn't it."

Then I sang, "O my God, nothing is hidden from you. You know all the grief of my heart. You know, Lord; you know."

"Yes, yes!" he cried. "That's it! That's the very song she sang!"

My friends, let's sing this hymn now, and then pray for the prisoners.

The "Afrikanka" is a special punishment cell. During my last term of imprisonment, I was put there three times, the last time for fifteen days. The floor of this small, cold cell is covered with four-inch iron spikes laid out checkerboard fashion, twelve inches apart, making it very hard to walk around and impossible to sit or lie down. An icy draft constantly blows in through the broken window. You can sleep only for a few minutes at a time, by squatting and leaning against the wall. But almost as soon as you fall asleep, you wake up again from the cold and have to start rubbing your arms and legs so you do not freeze. Prisoners who are put in this cell get so exhausted they eventually collapse and fall onto the spikes. That's why it is called the Afrikanka—you go in white and come out black, covered with bruises and dried blood.

It was only God's mercy and your prayers that sustained me and enabled me to endure the most difficult time in all my years of imprisonment. . . . The moment was critical. All my strength was gone. I remembered

Elijah, how he sat under the juniper bush and asked God to let him die. God did not grant his request. Instead he provided food and rest and then gave Elijah an assignment. I began to think, *Maybe God still has an assignment for me. It would be easier for me just to die, but is that what God wants?*

Just then I felt that the Lord's arms were around me, shielding me, and I heard God speak to my heart: "If you ask me for freedom, I will give it to you now without any compromises on your part. If you ask for death, I will let you die as my martyr. But if you pray, 'Thy will be done' and leave the decision to me, then I will continue to lead you in my ways."

Now a great struggle began. I knew with complete assurance that if I asked for either freedom or death, God would grant my request, with no dishonor or compromise on my part. But if I would yield myself completely to the will of God, I would continue to walk this path of suffering. I thought of Hezekiah, who expressed his own will and asked the Lord for fifteen more years of life. The Lord granted his request, but what happened as a result?

Do I have the right to demand anything from the Lord? I asked myself. Then I prayed, "Lord, I will make no more requests of you. May your will be done. Only give me the strength to do your will!" Joy suddenly flooded my heart.

After praying, I made my way over to the radiator, stepping carefully between the spikes on the floor. To my surprise, the radiator was warm! I leaned against it and warmed my back, and the pain began to subside. I realized that, as in the case of Elijah, a forty-day journey still lay ahead of me. How long this journey would actually last I didn't know, but it didn't matter anymore. I knew the Lord could free me at any time, but as long as I trusted him, he would lead me in the way that was pleasing to him.

Near the end of my five-year term, I felt I would not be released. When my family came to visit, they told me that Nikolai Baturin had been resentenced, and I was sure the same thing would happen to me. The camp authorities were putting a lot of pressure on me. They would not give me my mail, and the letters I wrote to my family were not getting out of the camp. I tried writing only brief, simple messages, but the administration still would not let the letters through. For instance, one of the officers told me I could write only what they allowed.

"Well, all right," I answered. "What shall I say? You dictate the letter, and I'll write it down and send it to my family so they'll at least know I'm alive."

"No," he said. "Even if we do that, you'll put in some secret message. Look, here's a letter you wrote. It says, 'I received the slippers you sent. Thank you. They are very nice.' There's some message in here."

"Believe me," I answered, "there's no secret message! My family sent me slippers, and I'm just letting them know I received them. That's all."

This is just one little episode, but there were so many other things. I began to feel there was no way out. I knew God always provides a way, but I just couldn't see any light at all. I felt as if I were in a long, dark tunnel. I kept telling myself that every tunnel has an end, that God would bring me out into the light again. Yet somehow my words sounded hollow.

Then one day I was summoned by an officer. "Come with me," he said. "The ground in front needs to be turned."

Two rows of barbed wire go around the camp, and the ground in between is constantly turned over so no weeds will grow there and footprints can easily be seen. The officer called another prisoner from my barracks, then took us to one of the soldiers and said, "Take these two men out front to dig."

We took our shovels and went with the soldier. He assigned us each a spot to work on, and we started turning the earth. He had nothing to do except guard us, so he walked over to me and started talking: "Hey, old man, what are you here for?"

"I'm a believer," I said. "That's why I was sentenced."

"A believer!" he exclaimed. "It can't be!"

"Haven't you ever met a believer?"

"Well, yes, I have," he answered. "What kind of believer are you?"

"I'm a Christian," I told him. "To be more specific, I'm a Baptist. Have you ever heard of Baptists?"

"Of course," he replied. "My neighbor was a Baptist. Here, let me see your name tag." He read my name. "Khorev? Wait, I know who you are! You're the one they write about in *Herald of Truth*."

Right then, the other prisoner started walking toward us. The soldier immediately sent him to dig at the farthest end of the fence. Then he told me, "When I was still living at home, before I was called up for military service, we had a neighbor who was a Baptist, the pastor of a church. He received *Bulletins* and *Herald of Truth*, but he couldn't keep them at home because his house was often searched. My parents let him keep the magazines at our house, and I read them all. That's how I know your name—I read the articles you wrote."

The young soldier had been drafted only four months earlier, so next he went on to give me all the latest news about the church that he had read in the magazines. We talked for three hours. Who could imagine that such a meeting was possible in camp?

"Did you ever go to a worship service with your neighbor?" I asked.

"I wanted to," he said, "but I decided against it because the police often show up at the meetings and take down everyone's name."

At the end of our talk, the young soldier said, "When you pray, please remember to pray for me, too."

"There's no need to put it off," I told him. "Let's pray now." So right there, shovel in hand, I prayed for him.

"I'll call you to dig out here again," he said as we parted.

But as it turned out, I never saw him again. The next day I was put in a punishment cell while a new case was prepared against me. Then I was taken back to court, resentenced, and transferred to another camp to serve two more years. I realized the Lord had sent this special meeting to encourage me. Our God arranges all our circumstances, and he knows just what we need and when we need it.

Today, on my first day at home, I remember the day exactly two years ago when I was supposed to be released from the camp at the end of a five-year term. Instead two more years were added. Yet I felt like a victor! My spirit was not broken! I thanked the Lord for my new circumstances and the amazing way in which he was leading me. I was sure the Lord had something special planned for the next two years. I sat alone in my cell—it was too small to walk around—and I sang the hymn "Rejoice, Rejoice, O Christian."

The guard by my door didn't try to stop me, but he asked, "How can you sing at a time like this?" He knew I should have been released that day. "A group of your friends are outside the gate," he said, "and they're all crying and worrying about you. How can you sing?"

Apparently my wife and son were waiting at the gate with Christian friends from Omsk and other cities. They had been told I would not be released, and they were grieving. This is how I tried to explain it to the guard: "Everything's just as it should be. They should cry, and I should rejoice. The one who bears the burden should be victorious, and the one who supports him should be concerned."

The apostle Peter provides a good example. While he was in prison, his spirit rejoiced and he slept peacefully. And the church? They stayed awake and prayed. Peter slept, and the church kept a vigil. Does it mean they were more spiritual? Not at all. It reveals their deep understanding of the situation. But Peter did not fear, even though he probably expected to be beheaded as James was. When the angel came into the cell, he had to wake Peter up. But what if Peter had been awake and worried, and the church had been sleeping peacefully? If another person is suffering need and hardship and you are calm and it doesn't touch your heart, then something is wrong.

On that day, two years ago, the Lord asked me a question. Of course, I didn't actually hear a voice, but in my heart I heard him ask, "Do you want anything special on the day of your release? Tell me your request."

I thought about it for a few minutes. *What do I really want? I want to be together with my whole family on the day of my release, which will also be my birthday. I want to pray with them on that day.* How could that be, though? Getting all the way home from Siberia in one day was practically impossible. Then when I was moved to Ulan-Ude, twice as far from home, I realized that the idea of meeting with my family on the day of my release was absolutely out of the question. Well, all right, I had expressed my desire to God; we have the right to do that.

Then unexpectedly, six weeks ago, I was summoned to the warden's office and told that I was being transferred to the prison in Kishinev. I asked why. The officer didn't know; he was only obeying orders. Guards were to accompany me to Kishinev by plane. Only then did I remember my request to pray with my family on the day of my release.

On November 11 I was handcuffed and escorted to Kishinev by three guards who said they had never heard of a prisoner being moved such a long distance by plane, only to be released in his home town. Usually prisoners are transported by train, and the trip takes weeks to months. What could I say? I just shrugged my shoulders. After this the soldiers didn't talk to me, because they are not allowed to. I was seated between them and couldn't talk to anyone else, which was fine with me because I could concentrate and pray to God.

I asked the Lord, "How am I worthy to be lifted to such a height?" I was not thinking of the plane's being thirty-three thousand feet in the air, but rather of the circumstances. Prisoners are never transported by air without an urgent reason. But in this case it was just for my release. The more I thought about it, the more certain I became that this was the answer to my request made two years ago. And today I can boldly say that we never ask enough of God. We limit him by our small expectations, as if we believe he is beyond our understanding.

I had asked God to let me be with my family today, on the day of my release, but his answer is much greater than my request. Not only can I pray with my family, but also with many friends who love and serve the Lord and his church. This is a day of celebration for all of us.

And just think—if this reunion is such a day of rejoicing, what will it be like when we finally reach heaven? We'll be reunited with all the saints who have gone before us, who have waited for us all these years. What a day that will be! And the joy of that glad meeting will never end. We'll have a lot to share with the saints waiting for us. We'll have much to rejoice about. And I think there will also be many surprises for us—because now we don't understand all the ways in which the Lord is leading us. I am not saying we'll understand everything the minute we arrive. I think we'll be learning to understand God's ways for thousands of years. We'll be filled with God's wisdom, and we'll be constantly delighted and amazed as we better understand the way he has led us. We'll say, "O Lord, how wise you are! We didn't understand so much."

Brothers and sisters, we need to trust God more right now. When we get to heaven, we will give him praise and glory. But, even now, God's goal in our lives is to teach us, even under extreme circumstances, to trust and praise him now as the God of all wisdom and glory. This is how he prepares us for heaven.

Several other ministers who were released ahead of me—Minyakov, Baturin, and others—were all put on probation, so I expected that I would be, too. But a prisoner can be placed on probation only if he has broken camp rules, which I had not, so I was curious to see what the camp administration would do.

Then, shortly before my release, the head prisoner in my barracks came to me and said, "Listen, Mikhail, I have to talk to you. The warden summoned me and said I have to report you for three violations in the next month. If I don't, he said he would put me in solitary confinement. What should I do?"

I didn't know what to say. Could I advise him to lie? But if I told him not to do it, he would be punished.

"I'm sorry," I finally said, "but I can't give you any advice. You'll have to decide for yourself."

"In that case, I guess I'll just put you down for minor violations, nothing you'll get put in solitary confinement for."

Sure enough, within a month, I had three violations on my record. So now I will be on probation for a year. What exactly this means I still don't know, except that I can't leave the city, I can't go out of my house in the evening, and the police will be checking to see if I am home. But in this, as in everything else, I'm trusting the Lord.

I see it this way: during the apostle Paul's years of ministry, he had little free time. He was always on the move, seldom in one place for long. It was hard to catch up with him. But when he was put under house arrest in Rome and couldn't go anywhere, everyone could go visit and talk to him. Paul wrote the Epistles during that time. So Paul's two years of "probation" were a blessing to everyone. I pray that, in the same way, God will use my year of probation as a blessing.

For the past several days, I have been thinking about seeing you all, and wondering what I should share with you. When I was on my way home today, it became clear. The main thought I want to express is this: The Lord never changes. He is the same yesterday, today, and forever, and until Christ returns, the church is constantly under his special care. If we are faithful to him in every circumstance, then we will experience his blessings. God will be on our side.

Mikhail Khorev's lively sermons make him a favorite with teens.

Twenty years have passed since the first time I was under investigation, since my first imprisonment. Ten days after that first arrest I was summoned to the investigator's office for questioning. For some reason, he left the doors open and seated me where I could see people walking by in the corridor. That was highly unusual; I wondered what was going on. Then I saw a guard and a prisoner walking by. The prisoner was Gennady Kryuchkov. He had just been arrested, and they wanted me to know it. This was a real blow. After he went by, the doors closed and the interrogation began.

"What do you think about that?" the investigator said.

"The president of your council is a prisoner. Your work is finished."

I answered, "If you were to tell me that you had crucified my Jesus again and buried him and rolled the stone over his grave, then it really would be the end. But Christ rose from the dead! So what can you say to grieve me?"

After he arose, Christ said, "Peace be unto you." And our Lord has not changed. He is still the same today. He gives us his peace in all circumstances—good and bad—no matter what.

Чаку Эмериц

с наилучшими

пожеланиями

V. Orbakat

Best wishes to you,

Charles Emert,

9

Vladimir Okhotin
Singer with a Captive Audience

Hey, Okhotin, we just got a call for you from the personnel office. You have to go by and sign your vacation forms," I was told.

Actually, I was already on vacation and had only stopped by work with my wife to pick up my pay. "All right, I'll go," I said.

"You'll go right over? You'll be sure to stop by the office?"

"Yes, yes, I'm going."

Being the music director of one's church may not seem like a subversive activity, but it was enough to get Vladimir Okhotin (b. 1942) a two-and-a-half-year prison sentence. Okhotin, then 42, was arrested in November 1984 for his ministry of music at the independent Baptist church in Krasnodar. He was released in May 1987. He and his wife, Nadia, are the parents of eight children.

137

When we reached the building with the personnel office, I noticed a black Volga parked on the corner. Right away I knew something was wrong. "I don't like that car," I said to my wife.

We entered the building, and the woman at the desk said, "Oh, good. We were hoping you would come. Take this form for your head engineer to sign, then bring it back here." To my wife she said, "You can wait here for your husband."

I took the form and left. As I stepped out the front door, I saw that the black Volga was now parked in front of the building. Two men standing beside the door grabbed me as I came out.

"Quick, get in the car!" one of them said.

"What's going on? Where are you taking me?"

"Don't talk. Just get in the car."

They shoved me in and climbed in beside me. During the whole ride, they held me firmly by my arms. First I was taken to the investigator's office, then to a jail cell at the police station. What a place it was: only three feet by six feet and full of bugs. They put a criminal in with me. "What did they pick you up for?" the other man asked.

"I'm a Christian," I told him.

"Well, I'll tell you what, if they don't find anything religious on you, they'll let you go." A few minutes later he was taken out again.

My first night in jail helped me prepare myself for what lay ahead. When your surroundings tell you that you have entered the front line of battle, you have to collect your thoughts and pray.

After a few days I was transferred from the jail cell to the prison. Everything there is metal—iron doors and bars—and it's so oppressive. The whole atmosphere weighs against a man's spirit, trying to crush him.

I was taken to my cell. First I greeted the prisoners; then I prayed.

"Who are you?" they asked. "What are you in for?"

I told them I am a believer, a Christian. Usually people in the criminal world know about Christians and respect them highly. Maybe not all of them, especially not the young ones, but those who have seen life have a great respect for believers and even try to help them.

From my first moments in prison I realized the Lord had brought me there to serve him. I was in bonds, but for a Christian, bonds are a new opportunity for ministry. How could I have a ministry there? By telling people about God, by preaching repentance. Some people will listen, but at the same time there are many adversaries.

The criminal world is held fast in Satan's cruel shackles. It's overwhelming to see the wretchedness of such people. I wanted so much to reach them, but mere words often seemed so futile. When I tried to talk to them about God, they would walk away. So I began to sing. To me, music has always been a way to serve God and give him glory. But while I was a prisoner, God gave me a whole new understanding of the ministry of music.

It is difficult to sing when people are talking loudly or occupied with other things. Such distractions affect a singer just as they would a speaker. And who expects prisoners in a crowded cell or noisy barracks to pay special attention to anyone? A prison cell may hold as many as seventy people, each one busy with his own affairs. Everyone is talking and no one is listening. What kind of ministry is possible in such a place?

The situation reminded me of Daniel, and I thought about how he carried out his ministry and worshiped God as was his custom. Daniel didn't try to get people's attention and seek an audience. He knew God had brought him to the palace to serve him. And Daniel's ministry included opening his windows facing Jerusalem and kneeling three times a day to pray for his people who were in captivity, exiled from their native land. He never looked to see if anyone noticed him, never cared about the praise of men or whether or not they paid attention to him. He knew that God heard him, and that was all that mattered.

I decided to follow Daniel's example and worship God as I always had. So, after I prayed, I started to sing. A hush soon fell over the cell. People were listening! I didn't have to try to get their attention and convince them to stop talking—the singing itself gave birth to quietness. It could only be God's power that made those people listen silently, because criminals don't respect anyone!

One of the hymns I often sang for them was "Remember, I'm Watching Over You." My dear friend Yakov Skornyakov loved to sing this hymn. He sang it many times while in the Rostov prison, and now I was singing it to my fellow prisoners. That hymn became precious to me in prison, and I wondered why I had not appreciated it before. I'm sure Yakov loved it so much because it reminds us that no matter what happens, God's eye is on us.

One day, as the seventy men from my cell returned from the exercise yard, I was thrilled when I heard a clear, strong voice sing out, "Remember, I'm watching over you. . . ." My heart overflowed as I prayed, "Thank you, Lord, that such words have reached the hearts of these men!"

Although many kinds of people are in prison, somehow they usually manage to get along reasonably well. On Easter Sunday I walked up to our "head" prisoner and said, "Today we celebrate the resurrection of Christ, and

I want to do something special. I would like to sing and worship the Lord. So would you please ask everyone to be quiet? They will if you give the order."

"All right," he answered. Then over the din he shouted, "Silence! Everyone be quiet. Vladimir is going to sing."

I began singing—for an hour, then two, then three. Finally I stopped and closed in prayer so as not to, as they say, wear out the audience.

More than anything else, I wanted the Lord to use my poems, my singing, and my words to touch the lives of these men so that my years in bonds might be spent sharing God's love. Singing was my ministry, and the Lord blessed it.

As I was moved around from one cell to another, the Lord used me to bear a testimony in many places. Finding myself in one cell, I would sing to the prisoners and tell them about God. Then I would be moved to another cell, where I had a chance to reach another group of people. Their first question to me was always, "What are you in for? What article of the Criminal Code?" I would answer that I was a Christian, then I would kneel and pray.

Of course, prison life was not easy for the flesh. Take tobacco smoke, for instance. I was in a cell with seventy people, and they were all smoking. The smoke became so thick I could barely see. Several times I nearly passed out for lack of oxygen. As a result, I was feeling weak the day my trial unexpectedly began. When the door opened, there I was, sitting in this smoky cell and feeling sick.

"Okhotin, come out."

I walked out to the corridor, and the guards started leading me somewhere. After a few minutes I asked,

"Where are you taking me?"

"Just be quiet and come with us."

"But where are we going?"

"To court," they told me.

"To court? Why wasn't I told in advance?"

"It's no big deal."

I was loaded into a police van and driven to the courthouse. When I stepped out of the van, I didn't even notice the fresh air because I saw my friends standing there waiting for me. I felt as if I were in a dream and thought I was seeing angels. How I rejoiced! How the Lord encouraged me through the presence of my friends!

Once I was in the courtroom a woman about thirty years old came over to see me and asked, "Are you Okhotin?"

"Yes, I am."

"I've been appointed to defend you. But I want you to reject me as your lawyer. Do you understand? How can I defend you? I'm a Party member. It would be easier to defend a murderer. None of us will defend you, so I ask you to reject me as your lawyer."

I told her I had already informed the investigator I would not accept any atheist lawyer. She seemed relieved and went to sit down. A few minutes later, though, she was back to ask again, "Will you please tell the judge you reject me?"

"Of course."

Five minutes later she came back again. "Now, you'll make it clear that you reject me, right?"

"Why are you so anxious?" I asked. "Of course I will."

The trial began, and the judge said, "Defendant Okhotin, you have the right to be assisted by a lawyer. What is your decision?"

I told him that the Bible declares the defense of man to be vain. God would defend me.

The judge then turned to the lawyer. "What is your opinion?"

"Of course, of course," she said. "Let the Almighty defend him."

During the trial I saw the Lord reveal his power and gain a victory. There's a portion of Scripture in Isaiah that I had never understood: "And I looked, and there was none to help; and I wondered that there was none to uphold: therefore mine own arm brought salvation unto me; and my fury, it upheld me" (Isa. 63:5).

I had always wondered what this meant—"My fury, it upheld me." But at the trial I began to understand. When I was brought into the courtroom and sat there across from the judge and his assistants, I realized this was combat. A battle to the death was about to begin. One would be victorious, and the other would be defeated. As a Christian, I knew I could not retreat. I had to gather all my strength for the battle, for I would either win or lose. No third option existed. David experienced this same fury when he went out to fight Goliath. He saw the Philistines ridiculing the people of God. They were reviling and blaspheming the name of God. How could David allow this to go on? Better to die than to accept such mockery.

If you are willing to accept a draw, if you will accept anything other than victory, you have already lost. The enemy will destroy you. You will be like Samson without his hair. Your outward appearance may be the same, but you will have no strength. And if you get to prison camp, you will have no boldness to preach to sinners. Sitting there, I experienced a feeling I had never known before. God gave me the strength that the moment required!

In addition, the Lord used a small incident to encourage me. Some of our friends were in the street outside the courtroom, and during a break one of them picked up my little two-year-old daughter, Maria, and held her up to the window so she could see me.

"Papa! Papa! Look at me!" she said and started to laugh.

Why is she laughing? I thought. *Her father has been taken away. She should cry, not laugh.* But then I realized it would break my heart if she cried. A verse in the Scriptures says, "He has filled my mouth with laughter," and this child's laughter encouraged me greatly.

Then she announced, "Now I will sing." She started singing, "On just such a quiet and holy night, God's Son was born to help us. . . ."

I was amazed. The Lord puts together all the little things in our lives and encourages us at just the time we need it. Little things are never little in the Lord's eyes.

After the first day of the trial I was taken back to the cell, and the prisoners greeted me like a member of the family. "How did it go, Okhotin? What happened?" They were concerned and wanted to know.

The next day I was taken back to court, and again I saw the Lord's power. He gave another great victory: the judge's two assistants were on my side during the trial. They always smiled at my answers. I could see them rejoicing at what I said. Their faces literally shone. But when they came back in with the judge for the reading of the verdict, I could hardly recognize them. Their faces were dark, and they kept their eyes down. They could not even look at me, and from their expressions I knew not to expect any mercy. The sentence would be just what the prosecutor had demanded. In spite of all the arguments, in spite of the total lack of evidence against me, I should expect no mercy.

When the sentence was pronounced, all the believers stood and sang the hymn "To Live with Jesus Is to Die with Him." Their singing was like a choir of angels. Their ministry was a bright testimony. People heard about their singing back at the prison and even later in the camp. One Christian girl even approached the prosecutor and started telling him about the Lord, trying to show him he was accusing me unjustly.

Good for her! I thought. *She came prepared to fight.*

I didn't join in the singing. I just listened, impressing it on my memory to take it with me. Then the believers started to throw flowers, which was also a testimony to the glory of God. I picked up a bouquet, but the guard snatched it away when he took me to the van. On the threshold of the van lay four carnations. I asked the soldier if I could take them with me, but he said no.

"May I at least have one?" I asked.

"Well, okay, just one."

I picked up a flower and put it under my coat. Then the guard locked me in the van. Outside, I heard soldiers talking among themselves.

"The flowers really belong to him," said one. "We should let him have them." A minute later, the door opened, and they handed me the other three flowers.

Back at the prison, I told the other prisoners about the trial and gave them the flowers. "Take them," I said. "They've already brought me greetings of love, and now they're for you." Those who had not been in freedom for a long time especially appreciated this gift.

Soon I learned that I would be transported to Camp #12.

"Oh, Okhotin," the others said, "that's the worst camp of all. It's a hungry camp." I prayed with them, shook their hands, and said farewell.

When I arrived at Camp #12, I couldn't believe my eyes. Compared to this place, prison had been beautiful. The camp was located in a swamp, so everything was always wet. What was worse, you could walk across the yard and see blood on the ground where the prisoners had brutalized each other. In the mess hall people were like beasts. We never got enough food, so everyone was hungry. And what's more terrifying than a hungry animal?

Hunger strangles the brain; it drives you wild with one desire—to eat. The prisoners beat each other and stole each other's food. Even if you did eat, it was never enough. After lunch, all you could think about was supper. After supper, you went to bed hungry and dreamed all night about breakfast. You think, *If I were free, I could fill up on bread. I wouldn't want anything else, just bread!*

One time I went into the commissary and bought a little bread. When I came back out, I found some tough prisoners waiting. "Give us the bread," they said.

Another man would have refused. Of course, being a Christian, I couldn't love them in word only. So I shared my bread even though I was famished.

Another time I was at work, and a large fire was burning below where I was standing. The smoke was really bad, and I had to breathe it. Soon it made me feel weak. But when the prisoners called, "Okhotin, sing us a song," I couldn't refuse and say the smoke was too bad. So I collected all my strength and sang, even with acrid smoke burning my throat and lungs. Of course, though some people wanted to hear, there was also opposition, as the apostle Paul said. We must sacrifice and fight for each soul.

Being a servant of the Lord in prison or work camp takes patience. You cannot rush things. Once you have announced you are a believer, the other prisoners watch you carefully. You must live a pure, Christian life. You are in corrupt, vile surroundings, but you cannot let the surroundings rub off on you. You must serve the Lord from your first day there. After I had been in the camp for about six months, one of the prisoners commented, "We don't know much about you, but we've been watching you. We see you're always clean and neat."

Prisoners notice cleanliness because they have to sit beside you in the mess hall and sleep in the neighboring bunks. Even in camp, if a person is tidy, he is respected. If he is slovenly, the others won't like him. Of course, staying clean in camp is easier said than done. When you wash your clothes, you have to sit and guard them until they are dry or they will be stolen. But people will not respect you if you don't take care of yourself and stay clean.

Never in my life had I fainted before, but I came close to it several times in camp. Losing consciousness wouldn't be so bad if it were just a matter of someone coming up from behind and hitting you on the head. But, when you feel your strength draining away and your body is struggling against falling, it feels awful.

At times like those, Satan stands right beside you, whispering, "It doesn't have to be like this. Your life could be different." He says that if you will just give in, just quit fighting and compromise a little, your life in camp can be better than at home. Some prisoners do have special arrangements with the authorities; they live

well, eating even butter and sausage. At such a moment
Satan offers you anything you want. As you struggle to
remain conscious, you can only whisper, "No, I don't
need anything from you." It is better to die than to accept
his offer. One must never give in, because this is the
beginning of compromise.

You must purpose in your heart not to defile yourself.
You must decide in advance that it is better to die than to
give in. This readiness to die is victory, for only then are
you really free. Nothing can alarm you. Your soul is with
the Lord, and you know God will provide everything. He
knows you need to eat, and he will send what you need,
even when you don't expect it. For instance, on one occasion when I was literally tormented by hunger, I felt I
could bear it no longer. I went to my barracks and there
on the night stand sat a package containing three rolls
with jam. I don't know where they came from. Apparently someone had come to visit and had left it for me.
God uses unexpected blessings to provide and lift our
heaviness.

The letters I received were also a blessing and great
testimony. What rewards there will be in heaven—for
Christ will say to many saints, "I was in prison, and you
visited me." The ministry of letters is a great source of
comfort and blessing to a prisoner, who longs for a word
from friends like one longs for water in the desert. One
Easter I received 136 letters and cards. As news of my
mail spread through the camp, people came to me asking, "Did you really get all that mail? How many friends
do you have? How many Christians are there, anyway?" I
did not keep my cards to myself but shared them with
others. Many people read them.

What kind of letters does a Christian prisoner need?
Primarily he needs the Word of God, because we do not

have Bibles in camp. One woman wrote, "Dear brother, I greet you in the love of our Lord Jesus Christ. I'm writing you chapter four of John." Then she went on to copy out the entire chapter and signed it, "With sincere greetings, your sister." It was so simple, yet so blessed. She took up her Bible and wrote. When anyone sends such a letter, that person need not worry about whether it will get through to the prisoner. That is God's business. All the sender must do is write.

I once got a card from a boy who wrote, "Dear Uncle Vladimir, I am eleven. I am in fifth grade. This is my message to you: 'Blessed are ye, when men shall revile you, and persecute you, and shall say all manner of evil against you falsely, for my sake. Rejoice, and be exceeding glad; for great is your reward in heaven: for so persecuted they the prophets which were before you.' Signed, Vasya." He is a wise boy! Though only eleven, he wrote such a good word of encouragement.

However, at one time I was feeling pretty discouraged. I went to the mess hall, where some people were ridiculing the truth, criticizing Christians in every way. So we had a confrontation. You cannot remain silent when people speak against the Lord. If you keep silent, you sin; you are giving up and giving tacit agreement to what they say. No matter what they do to you, you must defend the truth. When you do, you will have victory, and the others will respect you. They scorn a man who will not defend himself. But if you are not afraid of anything, if you can look them in the eye and tell the truth, they will respect you.

After this confrontation in the mess hall, an officer called me aside and said, "Okhotin, someone sends you greetings."

"Really? Who?"

"My mother," he said. "She's a believer. And not just from her. Her whole church sends you greetings."

The officer told me that his mother lived far away. He had gone to see her on vacation and told her about the Christian Okhotin in his camp. The news that she and the whole church sent greetings to me was like a message from heaven. My gratitude and joy were indescribable.

Being separated from other believers is a trial, even though we know God has reasons for sending people where he sends them. Camp administrators try to isolate Christians, surrounding them with people who curse and blaspheme. Only a person who knows the Lord is really able to help you and share your sorrows and griefs.

Any prisoner who shows kindness to a believer does so at his own risk. The authorities will put the squeeze on him until he stops, so I learned not to expect kindness from anyone. This strategy of the atheists explains why I was switched from one work brigade to another three times. My first supervisor liked me, so they moved me to another brigade. The second one started off hostile but changed his attitude when he got to know me. So I was moved again.

For two years I was alone. I often prayed, "Lord, please send one of the brothers in Christ here to me." Then the Lord sent me another brother, Mikhail Goryanin.

Mikhail and I always fasted on Fridays. We looked forward to Fridays because the spiritual power we received from these special times of prayer carried us through so many difficulties. So we fasted, even though we were sometimes punished for it.

We were also punished for not working on Sunday. I remember one Easter—it was made a "voluntary" work day. Mikhail was on the day shift, and I was on the evening. During the day, some prisoners said, "Okhotin, did you know your friend is in the punishment cell? He refused to work and was sent there for ten days."

After lunch that day, around two o'clock, the head of my work brigade told me to go to the office. I found several officers waiting for me there. One of them said, "Well, Okhotin, it seems you have quite a gift for poetry." (They had been reading my letters.) "So there's always a bright side, right? Good thing you were imprisoned so you could develop your talent." Then his tone changed. "We're ready to resentence you under a new article. We have all the evidence and witnesses we need. And next time, you'll get strict regime. What do you say to that? Are you ready to cooperate with us?"

"Don't bother trying to break me," I answered. "Do what you want. Don't talk to me."

This took them off guard. They are not used to prisoners' taking the offensive. When officials start hinting about "strict regime" camps and repeated terms, they expect prisoners to tremble and agree to anything.

"What do you think you're doing here anyway?" the officer continued. "Organizing a singing club? We've been patient with you, but our patience can end at any moment. You don't know how close you were to another trial. And what about Goryanin? What's he to you?"

"He's my brother in Christ."

"Well, he's in the punishment cell today. He wouldn't go to work. What do you think about that?"

"I'm ready to share his lot."

"Oh, you are, are you? Then you'll go there, too!" Then I got up and started to leave.

"Where are you going?" the officer asked.

"To the mess hall for lunch."

"Sit back down. We're not done." So I sat.

Then the major started to question me. "Listen, Okhotin, why should you have to go to the punishment cell? Just go to work."

"Not on Easter Sunday," I told him.

"Why not? Why should you be punished?" He tried to persuade me for a few minutes. Then they all changed their tactics and tried to scare me. When that didn't work, they started in with soft words again.

"Look," I finally said, "I've said all I have to say."

"Go ahead, then, get your head shaved."

I left the office. The next day I expected them to come for me during the morning roll call and take me to the punishment cell. But nothing happened. The following morning I again expected them to come for me. But again nothing happened.

I often thought about the subtle attacks Satan uses to cause a man to fall. For instance, the officers said I would not be able to see my family for refusing to work on Sunday. But the Bible tells us to keep "looking unto Jesus the author and finisher of our faith; who for the joy that was set before him endured the cross, despising the shame, and is set down at the right hand of the throne of God" (Heb. 12:2). When Satan comes with his subtle attacks, just fix your eyes on Christ, remember his wounds—and then all doubts will flee.

Mikhail and I were in complete agreement about not working on Sundays. And we could see how God helped us and took care of situations in advance. For example, one Sunday when I didn't go to work, I was summoned to the office and, on the way, ran into the head of Mikhail's brigade. When he saw that I was not at work, he seemed surprised and annoyed. As it turned out, Mikhail had not gone to work either, and this brigade leader had hoped *I* had, because the administration wanted to drive a wedge between us. They would have said, "See, you're both believers, but he went and you didn't."

This man accompanied me to the office. The officers there gave me a pen and paper and said, "Write out an explanation. What do you think you're doing in that brigade anyway, starting a choir? Here, write!"

"What do you want me to write?"

"Write an explanation of why you didn't go to work today."

So I wrote, "Today is Sunday, the Lord's day. This is why I didn't go to work."

They started discussing my statement. "Can't we force him to work?"

"No, we can't."

"Why not? We have the right."

"Well, actually, we don't. We can force him to work every day except Sunday." Then they noticed that I was still there and told me to leave.

Two months before the end of my term, two KGB officers came to see me. "Vladimir Okhotin," they said, "we're sorry you were sentenced."

"It's a little late, don't you think?" I said. "Where were you at the beginning of my term?"

"We couldn't help you then. We've only just now received authorization to offer amnesty to prisoners sentenced under Article 190-3. You and Goryanin can be released. You don't need to finish your terms. All you have to do is write a letter to the Presidium of the Supreme Soviet, requesting a pardon and assuring them that you won't commit similar crimes in the future."

The whole conversation was quite subtle. One of the officers started talking about some article he had read about the Shroud of Turin in a magazine. He began asking questions about Christ and the Bible, listening to the answers with apparent sincerity. But it was all a trick. After our talk, he said, "Go on to lunch, then come back again. I want to talk to you some more." But after lunch he said, "Now why don't you write that statement? And then you can go home."

This is how Satan attacks. I prayed for God to give me the strength to handle this matter correctly. A person can be faithful to God for many years but deny him in a hard moment. You have to remain on guard and always be careful. I told him I couldn't write such a statement.

"Why not?" he asked.

"You see, I'm not here as a criminal but for my Christian convictions. If I sign a statement saying I won't commit any more crimes, that's the same as saying I *have* committed crimes. It's an admission of guilt. But I'm not guilty, and I can't write what's untrue. All falsehood is sin. If you want to release me, do it without any conditions."

"Does that mean you won't sign?" he asked again.

"No, I won't."

"Then I guess that's it. Good-bye."

That evening I saw Mikhail. They had tried the same tactics on him, and he also had refused to sign.

A month later the public prosecutor came to see me. "Don't you want to write a statement requesting a pardon?"

"No, I can't request a pardon for crimes I didn't commit," I explained.

"Well, it doesn't have to be a request for a pardon exactly, just a simple statement that you won't continue to be involved with criminal activities in the future." So now they were trying to get me to write the same thing, only in different words!

Then, just before my release, the administration tried to pressure me into working on Sunday one last time. I still refused, so they said I would have to spend thirteen days in the punishment cell. Suddenly they pretended to change their minds. "Why is this necessary? You don't have to work. Just go to the work area and sit there."

"No, that's deceit. If I'm in the work area, that means I have to work."

"Then let's go get your head shaved. You're going to the punishment cell."

"Look, do you have to shave my head? I'm due for release in fifteen days," I reminded them.

"Too bad. If you don't sit still, we'll put you in handcuffs."

So they shaved my head and took me to a cell. I asked to be put in cell number six because Mikhail was there. The guard opened the door, and the prisoners started yelling, "Hey, we don't need any more."

But when Mikhail saw me, he said, "Please, come in, come in."

We embraced and prayed. I noticed he was thinner.

"Look, they shaved me," I said.

"Well, don't worry. The Bible says Jesus was like a lamb before the shearers."

We were together for exactly one day. As it has always been in the church, different people have different gifts. Mikhail was always the leader in preaching, and I in music. The other four prisoners would listen to him preach and then ask us to sing a duet.

The cell was cold and damp. The air in there was awful, too. Prisoners brew a super-strength tea that acts.

Vladimir Okhotin sang his way through prison camps. Since his release he continues to sing, direct choirs, and preach.

like a narcotic, and they burn whatever they can for the fire, usually rags. So the air was full of acrid smoke. The other prisoners in the cell were all young, so they could endure it, but it made my head spin.

The floor was bare cement. We had no blankets, mattresses, coats, or hats. I saw nothing for me to lie down on, only narrow, moldy benches. But one has to rest, so I asked Mikhail where we were supposed to sleep. Mikhail slept on a bare bench, and the rest of the prisoners— thieves—had each gotten hold of rags and cloths to lay on the floor. As a Christian, I could hardly ask them to share their stolen goods.

At first I tried copying Mikhail, sleeping on the narrow bench. But how could I sleep on such a bench? I spent the whole night trying not to fall off.

The next day was Mikhail's last day in the cell, and the others asked us to sing a last duet. Afterward he and I said good-bye. He knew my term was ending and that we would not be seeing each other in the camp again. He promised to climb up on the roof to see the friends who would come to meet me at the camp on my release day.

The next night I decided to try the floor. It was cold, wet, and crawling with wood-lice and cockroaches. After two hours I was frozen to the core. My back and kidneys ached so much that I had to get up again. So, for the next twelve nights, I tried to get some rest sitting up. It was still uncomfortable, but it was better than the floor.

The prosecutor came to see me once when I was in the punishment cell. "What are you doing here, Okhotin?" he asked.

"I'm here for not working on Sundays."

Suddenly he said, "So your main concern does not involve submitting to Soviet legislation on religious cults?"

"That's right. My only concern is submitting to the Word of God and obeying him."

"Well, all right. That's what I wanted to know."

I was really glad to hear him say this. It is good when our adversaries recognize that our main concern is fulfilling the Word of God. If we Christians keep this our primary goal, we will be strong, joyful, and victorious. If a person fails to fulfill the Word of God, he or she compromises and will be weak and full of shame.

My last really difficult test came on a Sunday night, my last night in the punishment cell. I was lying on the bench and was concentrating on not falling off. At about three o'clock in the morning, several prisoners in one of the other punishment cells escaped and made a dash back to the main camp. They were caught and brought back to the punishment block. When one of them was thrown into our cell, the other criminals grabbed him and started to beat him. They felt he deserved punishment for causing trouble. What was I to do? Such incidents happen in the camp, but if you get called on to report what criminals have done, what should you do? It is better to keep your eyes closed and pretend to be asleep.

But on this occasion I felt I had to do something. I prayed and asked God for strength. Then I started to stir a bit and got up as if I had just awakened. The others backed away from the man they had been beating. They looked a little ashamed and asked how I had slept. They wanted to be sure I had not heard what was going on.

At five, an officer appeared and said, "Okhotin, come on. Time to go."

I put my hands together to pray.

"What's wrong with your hands?" he asked.

"I'm praying before I leave, and then I'd like to sing a song."

When I said that, he looked nervous. He was not supposed to let me sing, but he looked around, saw no other guards, and said, "Okay, go ahead."

I sang a final hymn; then he took me to the guard house and told me I was being put on a transport. I asked if I could run back to the barracks.

"What for?" he asked.

"To get my jacket and hat, and I want to take my letters."

He accompanied me to the barracks. Everyone else was still asleep, so I didn't get to say good-bye. The officer really rushed me. He didn't even give me a chance to get my boots. Then he took me out to where a group of prisoners was waiting for transport.

"Where am I being sent?" I asked. "I'm supposed to be released on the twelfth."

"Just get on the train. You're going to Krasnodar. You'll spend the night in jail and be taken farther tomorrow."

I assumed I would be released the next day in Krasnodar. My only regret was that my wife was probably already on her way to meet me at camp. I prayed that when she got to the camp she wouldn't worry but would find out I had been released in Krasnodar.

We were loaded into the prison train car. We traveled to Timoshevsk, where the train stood at the station for twelve hours, then on to Novorossiysk, then to Krasnodar. All this time we were given nothing to eat or drink.

When we arrived, I was taken to the prison. Satan, the enemy of our souls, never stops trying to make us sin. The lieutenant colonel summoned me and said, "We're hoping you won't make any more mistakes and won't have to come back to prison again."

"A mistake didn't send me here," I declared. "I'm here because of my convictions."

As Christians our lives should be characterized by action and strength. If we say that the opinion of people around us does not matter, we are mistaken. Otherwise, why does the Lord say that we are the light of the world, the salt of the earth, that a city on a hill cannot be hidden?

Daniel was thrown into the lions' den because of the slanderous testimony and envy of worthless people. First, though, they had to demonstrate that he was a state criminal. But Daniel did not cry out or beg for mercy. When he landed in the lions' den, he knelt and prayed. What did God do? He sent his angel to close the mouths

ЛЯ МЕНЯ ЖИЗНЬ — ХРИСТОС

The Okhotin family is musical, too. The family gathers under a poster which reads: "For me to live is Christ. . . ."

of the lions. In the morning Daniel was brought out, and his enemies were cast in, but they cried out in terror because they knew they were guilty. It is the same way among criminals. But if your heart is clean, if you walk before God, you will not fear. God will send his angel.

10

Stepan Germaniuk
Exile at the End of the World

Before my trial, I was not held in prison. Instead the authorities let me live at home and continue working. The investigator simply called me in for questioning whenever he wanted me. He had a hard time building a case because there was no evidence against me. He could show only that I had preached at a number of church services and called people to revival. The investigator and I had an agreement, though: he promised that he would warn me when I was called in for the final interrogation, that is, when the authorities planned to arrest me.

Stepan Germaniuk (b. 1934) was forty-nine when authorities arrested him a second time in 1983 for his ministry with the CEBC, and for preaching the gospel in Voroshilovgrad and Kharkov. When Pastor Germaniuk was released from his second prison term in May 1986, his wife, Ulyana, did not welcome him home because she herself was imprisoned for her activities as a member of the Council of Prisoners' Relatives. Because of her deteriorating health she was released before completing her term, but died in July 1987.

One day at work the telephone rang. "Stepan," my co-worker called, "that man with the gruff voice wants to talk to you again."

I took the receiver and recognized the voice of Krucherov, my investigator.

"Stepan, come to my office immediately for a discussion," he said.

"Will I be able to leave after this talk?" I asked him.

"No, this time I can't guarantee it."

So I knew that this was it, that I would not be released. I told my fellow employees that I would not be seeing them again and bid them farewell. Some of them cried.

I went straight home, where I got my wife and children together. We knelt and committed our way into the Lord's hands. Our youngest child, who was then only three, started crying and begged, "Papa, don't go to the police!" I changed my clothes, packed some warm clothing and dry bread, and left with my wife. As soon as we got there the investigator showed me a warrant for my arrest and took me to the prosecutor's office. The prosecutor showed me three large files containing the materials of my case.

"Stepan Germaniuk," he said, "I know you well. All I need is one word from you—that you renounce all your religious activities—and I'll throw these three files into the fire and let you go free."

"I can't make such a promise," I answered. "I can't stop serving the Lord."

In tears, Ulyana and I said good-bye. I comforted her and said that the Lord would not forsake us. At that time we were hard-pressed financially. Our five children were small, and we had just put all our money into building a house.

When I was taken to the police station, I discovered

that my younger brother, Slavik, had been arrested the same day. We embraced each other and then knelt and prayed. The officer on duty did not try to stop us. Then we were led to separate cells.

While I was in the cell awaiting trial, the KGB conducted an experiment on me. They brought into my cell a man who was clearly insane. All day he babbled and shouted incoherent nonsense, but the other prisoners and I paid no attention to him. Toward evening the guards started summoning men out of the cell. There had been nine of us to start with, and seven were taken, so only this crazy man and I were left. I got really concerned. As soon as all the others were out of the cell, the other man tore off his clothes and started coming toward me. He was in a complete rage, and I could see that he planned to attack me in a filthy way. I started to pray and said to him in a loud voice, "In the name of Jesus Christ I order you to get away from me!"

He was a tall, strong man, but he immediately backed away. After a little while he started to close in on me again, and once more I ordered him in Jesus' name to get away. This went on for hours. I was tense and alert and prayed as hard as I could. I could not stop watching for even a minute because he would attack me. Later I learned that the prison administrators were observing the whole scene through a peephole in the door. They had evidently made a deal with this man beforehand that he would do this to me. But after I had repeatedly called on the name of Jesus Christ to order him away, and he helplessly withdrew to the corner each time, the authorities came in and took him away, naked as he was.

Then another strange man, very well dressed and wearing a hat, stepped into the cell, loudly criticizing the

Soviet government. Then he walked over to me and demanded, "Why don't you say anything?" he asked me.

"Because I obey the Bible," I answered, "and the Holy Scriptures clearly say that all authority is from God. As a Christian I can't speak evil of the government."

He tried to force me to say bad things about the government and would not leave me in peace. This went on all morning, but for me it was much easier than the previous night. The next day I was moved to my brother's cell.

The thought that my little children would be left without me grieved my heart. My greatest desire was that each of them should know and love the Lord. My brother and I decided that in addition to the regular day of prayer and fasting on Fridays, we would also set aside Wednesdays to fast and pray fervently for our families.

The trial, held in the large Voroshilovgrad courtroom, was basically a show trial. Lecturers from the local school and colleges were admitted, and a number of Christians managed to get inside. The prosecutor accused me of using my preaching as a cover for violating the legislation on religious cults. In my opening statement I showed that all the charges against me were false and contradictory. However, no attempt was made either to examine the charges or to determine whether my statement was true. Instead, the judges announced a recess. (Actually it was not a real recess. They just needed time to get more guards.) Afterward, my wife was the only Christian allowed back into the room.

Slavik and I refused to have lawyers. Instead we defended ourselves and spoke a great deal from the Word of God. We were fasting while the trial was in progress. This was on Thursday and Friday, the days of our Lord's suffering. On Friday afternoon everyone was allowed into the courtroom and the verdict was read: I was sentenced to four and a half years of camp, followed by three years of exile; and Slavik got four years of camp and two years of exile.

Right away, Christians began throwing flowers. I tried to pick up some that flew between the bars where I was sitting, but the guard grabbed me by the collar, tore the flowers from my hand, and shoved me out the back door. I did not even have a chance to pick up my bag and jacket; the police had to bring them to me later. In the meantime someone had locked the front door of the courtroom, trapping our friends inside so that they could not meet us at the prison van, but we heard them singing the song "Live for Jesus." It sounded wonderful.

I was sent to Camp #24 in Petrovsk, where I had a wonderful reception! My friend Pavel Rytikov was there, too, working as a shoemaker. He gave me some food and arranged a meeting for all the Christians in the camp to welcome me. He had a miniature Gospel, and for the next five months we met together to read and study the Word of God. When the day came for Pavel's release, I accompanied him as far as I could. I saw that a large group of friends holding flowers was waiting to meet him on the other side of the fence. The camp administrators were astonished to see how many friends we have!

Even in the camp the KGB never left me in peace. For over four years they continually tried to find a way to compromise me. For example, for a while I worked in a small office in the camp, filling out forms and distributing tools to the workers. My brother Slavik and two other Christians were in the same camp, and during break time we would get together in the office for a short time of fellowship and prayer. One time the camp administrator and a man in civilian clothes came into the office and asked for some paint. When I told them I needed orders from the warden, I noticed that the man in civilian clothes was carefully looking around the room, measuring it with his eyes. About an hour after they left, I suddenly felt compelled to go outside and look around. I walked around the building and spotted the same two men on the roof. I went back into the office, but soon I heard footsteps over my head. After lunch I asked one of the younger prisoners to climb up on the roof and see what was going on. He reported that a hole had been drilled in the roof, and inside it was a microphone with a wire coming out. From then on we were careful what we talked about.

On another occasion I was summoned to the warden's office. When I entered the room, I was met by KGB Lieutenant Colonel Romashka, who was wearing his military uniform. He stepped forward to greet me, held out his hand, and said, "Hello, Stepan!"

"It's against regulations to shake hands with a convict," I said without moving.

"What are you talking about. Forget that stuff!"

"No," I answered, "it's not allowed."

He sat down and invited me to have a seat. He had a traveling bag beside his chair, and he opened it part way so that I could see the food.

"So, Stepan," he said, "how are you doing?"

"Ivan Romashka," I replied, "I know why you're here. You've come to see if I've gotten weak. First you give me a severe sentence, and now you come along with a bag of food to see whether I'll give in and take your hand and say, 'Please help me get out of here!' Just leave me in peace. It would be better for me to die in prison than to accept any help from you."

Sometimes the KGB would suddenly show up to

check on us. They criticized the camp authorities for letting me have a good job and demanded that I be assigned to the hardest work. One time I was transferred to a section where the prisoners melted tar. The fumes were noxious. But I learned the job, tried to work well, and sang to myself. Several times the warden came to see how I was doing, and finally he moved me back to lighter work.

There was one particularly joyful incident in Camp #24. It concerned a political dissident in our camp, a very broken, despondent man. He spent all his free time with books, reading and searching for some eternal meaning in life. I had many opportunities to talk to him about God, Christ, and the salvation of his soul. One day he met me in the yard and said, "Stepan, please help me. I want to pray!" We went into the empty workshop, and he fell on his knees and began to weep. He prayed to God, asking that his sins be forgiven. I could see that his repentance was genuine. That evening I told the other Christians that this man had repented. We rejoiced so much! He was due to be released soon. Afterwards I received word from freedom that he was standing firm in the faith.

Toward the end of my term, before I was sent into exile, KGB agents started coming to the camp to talk with me. One time I was summoned directly from work and had no chance to wash my hands. When I came into the office, the two agents held out their hands to greet me.

"I'm sorry," I said, "but as you can see, my hands are dirty. I've just come from work."

"Is that so?" they asked. "And if your hands were clean, would you shake our hands?"

"No, I wouldn't offer you a clean hand either," I admitted.

"Well, at least you're frank."

"Who are you, anyway?" I asked.

"We're just people who've come to talk to you."

"If I don't know who you are, I won't talk to you." I turned to leave.

At this point they showed me their identifications. One man was KGB Major Fesunenko from Kiev and the other man, who was older, was KGB Colonel Ivan Volynyuk from Voroshilovgrad. During our conversation they explained that they were working to unite the AUCECB ["registered Baptists"—see glossary] with the Council of Evangelical Baptist Churches (CEBC) and in general were working toward the joining of all religious denominations at an international level.

"Why should anyone want to call himself either Baptist or Orthodox when all the churches can be one?" they asked, adding that they wanted to help us all get together.

"I'm still a prisoner," I said, "and I have three years to go. I don't have anything to do with these matters. But if you want to know my personal opinion, I'm categorically opposed to any such union."

So they started talking about my family and how sad it was that my children had to get along without me for so many years. They said that my freedom depended on whether I would cooperate with them. However, I replied that nothing depended on them, that everything in my life came to pass exactly as God had ordained it, and that God took care of my family and provided everything they needed. In conclusion I said that I would not accept any help from them. Then they left.

The day before my sentence ended, my wife came to the camp and we were granted a short visit. I told Ulyana that I was being exiled to Khabarovsk krai, very far from our home. She had brought me food for the journey, and we said good-bye.

The other prisoners gave me a farewell party. Many people had gotten to know me and treated me with respect. I had spoken to many men about God, and at our parting I preached to them again and asked them not to forget our many conversations. "Yes, Germaniuk," they said, "we'll remember. But we'll never meet another man like you." I learned later, however, that soon after I left, the Lord sent them Aleksandr Krugovikh, a preacher from Makeyevka.

I did not really know what the conditions would be like on the transport to my place of exile, but I had a feeling it would not be easy. I was right. The transport started at the Voroshilovgrad prison and ended thousands of miles to the east at Nikolaevsk-na-Amure. I passed through nine hard prisons, traveled in many prison cars with hundreds of convicts, covered a large part of the territory of the Soviet Union, and witnessed all kinds of violence and hardship.

On the trains the guards would lock seventeen to twenty prisoners in a cabin meant to hold four, and we would travel like that, usually for four days at a stretch. In the prisons they would give us food for each leg of the trip—some small salted fish and a hunk of black bread. The prisoners usually sat down on the train platform, ate all their food at once, and then went hungry for three days.

The transport will always remain very memorable for me because even though it was an awful experience, it was at the same time simply saturated with God's blessing. During the trip I had many good conversations about the Lord. People were very interested in hearing about God.

The first prison of the transport, the Voroshilovgrad prison, is absolutely filthy, full of lice, other bugs, and dirt. I spent several days there, my "home prison," and then was taken by train to Kharkov. The transfer prison in Kharkov is a massive place. There they were not satisfied with the service we had received at the Voroshilovgrad prison. They scalded us to kill off the bugs, then put us in a halfway decent transport cell.

I remember meeting a toothless prisoner there named Jan. He had been in prison for twenty-seven years. During his last term he had tried to escape and as a result was sentenced to several more years. Jan had no faith in anything. But when I recited Dershavin's poem "God" to him, he listened very carefully, with tears welling up in his eyes.

"I don't listen to anybody or anything," he said. "I don't believe anyone, but here you come along with your poem about God, and somehow you've touched my heart."

For several days Jan stuck very close to me, but then we were separated and taken in different directions. I don't know what ever became of him. It is pitiful to see such people and so sad to part with them when you feel as if you have somehow held them back from the brink of despair.

After six or seven days in Kharkov, I was sent to Sverdlovsk, where the prison is a horrible place and very large. For several nights on the train we had not been able to sleep; but when we got to this prison, they put us in a tiny metal cell instead of a regular cell. The prisoners started to demand that we be moved, but one of the women working there said, "Listen, fellows, you'd be better off staying where you are. The stealing here is so bad that they'll take everything you've got. Besides, you're being shipped out tonight."

They fed us some soup that was actually still warm, and it gave us a little strength. That evening we were loaded back onto the train.

The next prison was in Novosibirsk and, in my opinion, it was much cleaner there. They fed us and gave us some extra food for the trip to Krasnoyarsk.

The prison at Krasnoyarsk is an old wooden building. They unloaded us into the basement and gave us each something that was supposed to be a mattress. I don't know how many people had died on my mattress, but there was hardly anything left of it. Then they took us to a cell that had dried blood on the floor and walls. It was obvious that prisoners had been beaten in there, maybe even killed. One night I was moved to a cell on death row. The chairs there were cemented to the floor, and there was an iron table. Heavy iron bars covered the little window. It was a dark, depressing place.

After a stay in Krasnoyarsk, I was transported to the prison in Irkutsk, and I can scarcely describe what a loathsome place that was. It is a three-story building, and you get from one floor to the next by using metal ladders, like a fire escape. Because we were absolutely exhausted when we arrived in Irkutsk, as soon as the guards locked us in the cell we collapsed onto the beds. But before we could fall asleep, prisoners started yelling and jumping up from the bunks because of the hoards of insects that began pouring out of the seams of the mattresses and biting us viciously. These were some kind of blood-sucking parasite, and they were having us for supper. We found some cans and spent the rest of the night catching bugs.

The next morning we told the guards we refused to eat until they moved us, asking why they had put us in such an awful cell. The prison doctor was summoned, and he said, "Come on, cut out your lying! There aren't any bugs in here." As proof, we showed him all the ones we had collected during the night. He could hardly believe his eyes, but he had us moved immediately, and all our clothes had to be scalded.

On the train that brought us to Irkutsk I had met a political prisoner from Leningrad named Egor Davydov. He was a pretty good person. I never heard a bad word from him. He stuck close to me and slept beside me at night. He really treated people well, and he was different from many of the prisoners. Davydov had been imprisoned for ten years. He was very interested in our brotherhood and wanted to know more about Christians. I tried to show him that his political struggle was leading him nowhere. I encouraged him to become more closely acquainted with God, telling him that when a man knows God, he has something that is truly worth living and fighting for. We parted in Irkutsk, because it was there he was staying for his exile. Egor not only kept in touch and wrote me from exile, but he also contacted my family and gave them news about me.

After staying in Irkutsk awhile, we were taken on to Khabarovsk. The prison in Khabarovsk is also very bad. But is there such a thing as a good prison? In this place, though, for some reason we were not searched until the next morning. We were all put into one big cell and left there totally unsupervised. No guards checked on us. I won't even try to describe the violence that I saw that night!

I was taken from the Khabarovsk prison in handcuffs. The guards said they were taking me to Nikolaevsk-na-

Amure by airplane and warned me not to talk or turn around or do anything but just sit quietly in those handcuffs. When they put me on an AN-24, a passenger plane, the regular passengers looked me over. I was pale and tired, and my beard had grown out during the long transport. Two soldiers sat behind me, two others sat in front, and an officer from the Department of Internal Affairs sat beside me.

When I arrived at the prison in Nikolaevsk, I was given a friendly welcome. They gave me some good fish soup and real bread, not the half-baked nasty stuff you usually get in prison. The prison there is small—and of course the less food they have to prepare, the better it is. The place was very pleasant and had a homey smell. I was able to rest there for two days. Then I was told that I would be sent to Chumikan for exile.

What's Chumikan? I wondered. *Some obscure little village at the end of the world?* But I got ready to go.

A political prisoner named Mikhail Sidov traveled with me from Nikolaevsk. Without any guards, we were put on a little AN-2, a crop duster. When the plane landed in Tugura and we got out, there were no police around. Since we had gotten used to being constantly surrounded by police, we were confused to find them gone.

"Maybe we got off at the wrong place," Mikhail suggested.

We walked around the airport, not knowing what to do. We were afraid that someone would suddenly grab us and accuse us of trying to escape. Finally we went to the dispatcher.

"You've arrived, fellows," he smiled. "This is the village of exiles. Don't expect anyone to meet you here. There are no buses, and the village is four kilometers from here, so you'll have to walk. Go to the police station in the village, and we'll send your files over."

We went back outside, where the wind was raging. There were only a few trees, small and deformed. We had heard that it is always cold there and that there are constant snowstorms and blizzards.

Of course, I had not expected that exile would be a vacation. However, the Bible says, "[They] meant it for evil, but God planned it for good." So I took off my hat and prayed aloud, "The earth is the Lord's and everything in it, and if there are any people living here, if there is even one, then I can live here, too. I'll glorify you in this place, my Lord."

Mikhail and I started to walk toward the village, but he got so cold that he could not stand the wind. I gave him my hat and padded jacket, and together we continued on to the village. As we approached it, we saw dogs everywhere on the streets, more dogs than people.

Chumikan is a tiny village, lost far away in the taiga, and you can get there only by airplane or by one of the barges that come to bring food and coal in the summer. The village is situated where the Uda River flows into the Sea of Okhotsk. This little village, in the northern part of Khabarovsk krai, is about as remote as you can get. You can go no further. I found myself over six thousand miles from the camp where I had served my term. It was a pretty dismal spot.

When Mikhail and I finally walked into the village, we were almost frozen. We went to the police station and announced our arrival. The police chief said, "Okay, just wait here awhile. When your files arrive, I'll talk to you." Then he added a word of warning to me. "Don't think that you're going to do any preaching here. We won't allow it. We're very strict."

"And what punishment will you give me that's stricter than sending me here?" I asked. "Do you plan to send me south? I'm a preacher by my convictions and my calling. So I'll preach." But then again, I realize that it's his job to give such warnings.

When the files arrived, the police chief assigned us work and let us go. Next we went to the regional office, where two women were sitting at desks, writing. I stepped up to one of them, announced that I was a Christian, a man who believed in God, and that I had been sent into exile for my faith. Everyone in the room looked up and listened. This was something new for them. For as long as the village had existed, there had never been any believers sent there for exile.

I was assigned to a dormitory in the village. The place was absolutely filthy, and everyone was drunk. I heard that one man who lived there would get paid and then go buy vodka and something to eat. He would get drunk, pass out, wake up again and drink some more, on and on until his money was gone. That was the general situation in the dormitory—unrestrained sin and terrible drunkenness.

Leaving Mikhail there, I decided that I was not going to stay in that dormitory for a single day. I went back to the office and asked the women to find me a room in somebody's house. We started going door to door, but no one would take me; they were all afraid of exiles. In their way of thinking, an exile is a scourge. Finally we came to the house of an elderly lady, a Mordvinian, and asked her to take me in.

"No way!" she replied.

"But listen, grandmother, I'm a man who believes in God. Let me stay in your house. I'll help you. You won't regret taking me in."

"Well, all right," she said. "As long as you believe in God, I'll take you. But not today. Come back in four days, and I'll have a place ready for you."

So I checked into the motel. Then I decided to go to the dormitory and visit Mikhail. I found him sitting on his bunk, hunched over and shivering. "They brought me here to die," he said. "There's no way I can survive here. It's cold, and there's nothing to eat. I know I'll die."

"No, you won't die," I told him. "How much money did they give you?"

"Ten rubles."

"Okay, come with me."

We went to the store, and I bought him a hot plate for four and a half rubles. Then I bought some macaroni, dried milk, ingredients for soup, a loaf of bread, and a few other things. We went back to the dormitory, turned on the hot plate, and cooked some macaroni soup. As the soup smell spread throughout the room, he cheered up. A man really needs very little to cheer him up and keep him alive!

A few days later I moved in with the elderly woman, who had even prepared a bed for me. I knelt beside the bed and prayed aloud, thanking the Lord that he had given me this place to stay.

I wrote home to my wife and described the situation in Chumikan, how hard it was just to get enough food, and I told her that I would not see her until the end of my three years of exile because there was no way she could get to this place. I wrote the letter in November, and in December my wonderful wife flew into Chumikan! She had gone to see Lydia Vins, told her where I was, and let her read my letter.

"Ulyana, go to him immediately," Lydia advised. "Go right away. Don't worry what anyone else says or thinks;

you just go and see for yourself." So my wife got on an airplane and came to see me.

The airport notified me that my wife had arrived, but I couldn't walk there because we were in the middle of a bad snowstorm, and everything was buried by snow. Borrowing a car from work, I drove to the airport to get Ulyana. As soon as we got to my landlady's house, we immediately knelt to thank God. After we prayed, Ulyana said, "You wrote that you wouldn't see me here, but in less than two months, here I am!" Four days later she returned home with the firm intention of moving to the village in the spring.

After that, my life went on as before. My landlady was enslaved to drunkenness. She worked three jobs, earning up to five hundred rubles a month and spending all her money on liquor. When I moved into her house, I pleaded with her to give up drinking. Her friends stopped coming over, and she remarked, "Look at this, I've got a holy man living in my house."

Before long, though, things started to change. I washed and scrubbed everything and got the place into order. I also cooked good Ukrainian food for her, such as borscht. Because of all my help, she didn't even charge me rent. My friends sent me a lot of food packages, and praise God, she and I lived well.

In April of the next year, 1978, my wife and children arrived in Chumikan. The authorities had promised to give us our own apartment. By this time I was working as a head bookkeeper. My supervisor had grown to like me pretty well, and he saw to it that I got a good place.

However, when the local Party committee found out that I had gotten an apartment, they decided to kick us out. The girls had already hung curtains, and we had sung hymns and blessed the place with prayer, but the superintendent came and evicted us. Instead they made us move into an old rat-infested building. But we carried in our bags, sat down on them, got out the guitar, and sang and praised God. Everyone was optimistic and happy; we knew God would provide something.

Soon afterwards I got permission from my work supervisor to buy a shack near the forest for eighty rubles. After that my supervisor sent some people to get the place fixed up, we added a couple of rooms, and in a month the house looked wonderful. We praised the Lord. When the head of the local Party committee heard about the house, he said, "Look, this Baptist has tricked us. Even here he has paradise."

Near the house I planted a small garden. I planted potatoes in stones, the only way they will grow that far north, where the summer is only two months long. The sun heats the stones and the potatoes grow, even though they come out deformed. We had enough for the whole winter.

Before long, we became friends with another family that lived nearby. I visited them often and found out that the father had died many years before for preaching the gospel. I also learned that the family had known Eugene Rodoslavov, a Christian who was in exile in a nearby village, Bogordskoe. Through his testimony, several of their family members had come to know the Lord. However, the oldest brother, Ilya, was very stubborn and refused to accept Christ for a long time. His wife was one of the women working in the village office. When I had first arrived in the village and announced that I was a Christian, she had gone home and told her husband, "This believer was probably sent here for our sake." At first Ilya asked, "Why didn't you invite him over?" But then he added, "Oh, well, I'm sure we'll run into him anyway."

As it turned out, I did meet them soon afterward, because the elderly woman in whose house I had lived knew them. Once when they were visiting her, I was able to talk to them for several hours. Later I started visiting them often, and they also came to see us. Ilya was a fisherman, but his wife was an educated woman, an economist and a bookkeeper. For many years she had tried to keep him from coming to the Lord, but now the Lord had touched her heart, and she was urging her husband to repent. What a joyful occasion it was when both of them were saved in our home! How they wept, and what joy we had in the Lord!

Our worship services in Chumikan were wonderful. Sometimes on Sundays our meetings would last from morning to evening. We sang hymns and worshiped God all day long. I spent much time in prayer and in the Word so that I would have something to feed the people. We always began with a time of prayer. At each service we read several chapters from the Old Testament and several from the New Testament, trying to get through the whole Bible. Our daughters Lilia and Olga took a very active role in our services. They played the guitar so that we could sing. And the little ones participated with their poetry. We sang a great deal at the services, knowing that people who are newly saved really need to sing. We had some good handwritten song books, and we would sing for hours, hardly noticing the time passing. I don't think we will ever again know such fellowship on earth.

We discipled Ilya and his wife; and when the summer came, I baptized them in the frigid saltwater of a lake beside the sea. The Lord greatly blessed that baptismal service. It may have been the first time that anyone had ever been baptized in that stark region, the first time that people testified that they believed in the Lord and had given their lives to him. We had a big celebration and a special meal. I laid hands on them and prayed. Then we shared communion. There was so much joy in our home and especially in the hearts of these two people who had found forgiveness. The prayers of Ilya's parents, who were both committed believers, had not gone unanswered.

Our family spent a lot of time with Ilya and his wife, and we saw them growing spiritually every day. Their youngest son, Tolik, became a friend of our children and learned a lot from them. We enjoyed this fellowship very much but knew that soon we would have to part.

By this time the local authorities had become concerned about us. The head of the local Party committee called me into his office and said that we were forbidden to gather anymore. He warned, "You'd better watch out, or we'll take care of you."

I talked to him pleasantly, telling him that I was not afraid of their threats and that I would continue preaching because this is God's will.

Not long after this I was summoned to the police station. The police showed me a warrant to search my house, supposedly for sable pelts. (In this part of the country many people hunt sable and sell the pelts.) I told them to go ahead, but I realized that they were looking for something else. I went home and told my children that there would be a house search, so we knelt together and prayed about it. Soon four policemen arrived and began searching. As soon as they found some Christian literature, they set it aside for confiscation.

"Don't take that," I said. "It's not sable."

"We're taking it anyway," they answered.

So I demanded to see the prosecutor. They sent one of the men to get him, and when he arrived, he seemed quite upset and said, "I don't know anything about this. I've never had to deal with this before. I'll check with Biriukov."

(Biriukov was the KGB chief. This little village had no KGB agents before I was exiled there. But two or three months after I arrived in Chumikan, KGB agent Gennady Biriukov was sent out. He summoned me only a few times for talks and for the most part observed me from a distance. Apparently he had been ordered not to talk to me.)

So now the prosecutor was saying, "I'm not informed on this matter. I'll go see Biriukov and do whatever he advises." A few minutes later he came back and said, "Confiscate everything that mentions God. We'll check it and then return it."

Nevertheless God continued to bless us. The children and I decided to memorize one chapter from the Bible each week. On Wednesdays our family always fasted, and the children knew that no matter what, we would always have a service on Wednesday and recite our chapter for the week. Sometimes we had to peek, but we usually knew our chapters by heart. To this day the children can remember many of the chapters they learned, especially from Isaiah and the Epistles of James and Peter.

The children and I loved to walk along the seashore and watch the roaring waves or the silent stars. The sky in the Far East is very unusual. In the Ukraine the sky seems very high and the stars so small, but out there the stars were so big, and we could never get our fill of gazing at them. Often at night we would go out to watch the stars and would sing the song, "O starry sky, what a marvel you are, what a reflection of God's love!"

We had a great desire to leave a testimony in this place. I remember how, at four o'clock one Easter morning, I went outside and walked through the streets shouting, "Chumikan, listen! Christ is risen!" Of course, some people were more interested than others. The wives of the policemen and other local officials showed particular interest. I gave them a little book to read entitled *Is There Life Beyond the Grave?* I witnessed to them in other ways, too. I especially witnessed to the elderly woman in whose house I had first lived, but she and her children were still enslaved to drunkenness and debauchery.

My family never felt alone, even in that remote village. We heard from people in Zakarpatie, the Caucasus, Murmansk and Central Russia, Siberia, the Urals, and Asia. There was not a single corner of the country from which we did not receive cards, letters, and packages. We tried to answer everyone who wrote, even if only with a few short lines. When I was in the camp, it was impossible to answer all the mail I received, so from exile I made it a point to answer everyone. And what an amazing blessing it was to receive those letters! It was wonderful to learn how things were going with our Christian friends in Moscow, Odessa, Kharkov, Kiev, and our own home town, Voroshilovgrad.

My term of exile ended in June 1980. I received my passport, and we loaded our belongings onto a barge and prepared to leave. Even my boss came to see us off. We had become good friends, and I had often talked to him about God. As the barge prepared to sail, I walked out on the deck and prayed to God. I thanked him for this village and prayed for his blessing to abide there, and I thanked him for sheltering me and caring for me in that place. Then I said good-bye to Chumikan, knowing that I would probably never see it again.

Three years of exile had passed. What had I learned? I try to take a lesson from everything that happens in my life, from each prison term and from each place I live. And there in Chumikan the Lord taught me to hope in him at all times, just as it is written in Psalm 62:8, "Trust in him at all times; ye people, pour out your heart before him: God is a refuge for us." And truly we had everything in abundance there—we had enough to eat, and all our other needs were met. We saw God's constant care and provision.

But the greatest joy of all in Chumikan was to baptize in those cold waters people who had turned to the Lord. It was so precious for us to hear them say, "Thank you, Lord, for sending this family here." For, indeed, God had sent us, and we fulfilled our mission. We did his will, and we learned the lesson of trusting in God at all times; for, no matter what the circumstances, he is always with us.

God was with us even there in the taiga, where the winter temperatures dropped to $-49°$ Fahrenheit and the wind sometimes blew fifty miles per hour, knocking people off their feet and ripping the roofs off houses. He was with us when the blizzards were so severe that we could not go outside for fear we could not find the house again. He was with us when the children had to stay at school for several days because they could not get home. Living in such a place makes a man's heart softer and kinder. Praise God that all the storms we encountered, all the moving and changes of housing, and all the house searches were foreordained for us by him. For this reason alone we should thank God, thank him for everything.

Exile is a very good school for a person who wants to learn something from God. The whole earth is the Lord's! Everything belongs to God—the promises, the revelation, and the people. We were living among

Evenks, Yakuts, Tunguses, and Nanaians. These tribes are becoming extinct, and they are perishing without knowing God, but God gave me an opportunity to speak to them, to live among them, and make known to them the name of the Lord.

While I was serving God in these places of imprisonment and exile, I sometimes wondered, "Where will the Lord send me to serve him next? Where will the Almighty use me?" While in Chumikan I prayed very much that the Lord would show us where to go when the time came to leave. My wife had sold all our possessions, so we really had nothing to return to in the town where we had lived before. Our children were growing up and needed to be in a good church with a youth group, music, and a choir. We decided to go to Kharkov.

When we arrived in the Kharkov district, the ministers gave me a warm reception. They asked me about my past ministry and then included me in the district council and the leadership of the local church. My whole family was involved in evangelism. Our children, too, became members of the Dergachevskaya church, which is a very good, healthy congregation. They have an excellent senior pastor, Viktor Mosha, a very experienced minister. At that time he had served three terms of imprisonment, and now he is in bonds again for the fourth time.

The local authorities were hostile from the start. Soon after we got settled, they came to break up a worship service, and I was imprisoned for fifteen days. By the end of 1981 I had served four fifteen-day sentences for attending worship services. Then they started preparing a new criminal case against me. On May 8, 1983, I was walking to the place where a service was to be held when suddenly two men jumped out of a side street and grabbed me. They seized my briefcase, showed me a document from the KGB, pushed me into a car, and drove me away.

In my cell I was excited to see two Bible verses—Revelation 2:10 and 1 Corinthians 10:31—penciled onto the rough walls in the distinctive handwriting of my friend Pavel Rytikov. He and I had served the Lord together in the churches in the same district, and we had also been imprisoned together earlier. I knew that he had been arrested in March, but of course he did not know that I had been, too. Now I knew he was in this same prison somewhere. I was assigned a *troinik* cell and led there down a corridor. As I walked, I saw another prisoner ahead of us. As I got closer, I saw that it was none other than Pavel Rytikov!

We talked fast because we expected to be separated at any moment. Instead the guards took us to the basement and put us into the same cell. As we walked through the door, Pavel stepped on my foot to warn me that there was a "plant" in the cell, so we had to be careful of what we said. We did most of our talking when we were taken out to the exercise yard. We also spent time praying together. Three days passed very quickly, and then Pavel was taken to court, and I did not see him again.

I remained in this cell, where I was able to talk to the other prisoners a lot about God. No one interfered or tried to stop me. In the course of six weeks I told them everything I knew from the Old Testament, including the prophecies about Christ. Then I talked about the life and crucifixion of the Lord. Some of the men had been raised in orphanages and had never heard anything about God, so for them this was all new. Whenever I spoke about God, the other six or seven prisoners would listen attentively and then discuss what they had heard.

During the investigation of my case, the authorities rarely summoned me for questioning. After all, what point would there have been? I was accused of violating Article 187 of the Ukrainian Criminal Code: knowingly spreading slanderous fabrications about the Soviet government and society. But they had no evidence against me.

On the eve of Easter I was still in the cell. Instead of a celebration it was a time of sadness. There was a stone in my heart, which was sealed with sorrow, but I was not too discouraged. I had been prepared for this—I had known that I could be arrested at any time. The following day all my friends from church came to the prison after the morning service. Thereby the seal was broken and the stone was cast away from my heart, just as the stone was cast away from the tomb. My friends had come! I could hear them singing and see them from the window of my cell. There were so many that the police were alarmed, and they had me transferred to a different prison the same day.

That was how my second term of wandering and imprisonment began. I was sentenced to three years' strict regime. But I felt in my spirit that our enemies were still not satisfied. It was not enough for them to deprive me of freedom, to separate me from my wife and children. They were preparing another attack, which came when they arrested my poor, tired, ill wife, Ulyana.

Ulyana was arrested while taking our sons to school. The police took her off the train, falsely accusing her of leading the congregation in Kharkov. At first she was sentenced to fifteen days. Our children wrote and told me about this. Then the court indicted Ulyana on Articles 187 and 138 of the Ukrainian Criminal Code and sentenced her to three years of imprisonment. Our chil-

Stepan and Ulyana Germaniuk at the wedding of their daughter Lila to Ivan Khorev in May 1987. Ivan's mother is on the right. Ulyana's condition had deteriorated so much that she was released from prison in March. On July 3 she died of stomach cancer.

dren were terribly upset. They could hardly stand to hear all the slander and evil lies in the indictment against their mother, and they were also very worried about her health. It was in this sorrowful and hopeless condition that they wrote me and said, "Papa, now Mama will be where you are."

So my wife was in bonds and my children were alone. Atheism is very cruel. *What will the atheists do to us next?* I wondered. And what can atheism offer to anyone? They were conducting an experiment against our family by imprisoning both parents and leaving the children alone.

But thanks be to God, by this time all our children were members of the church. We could face suffering with peace in our hearts because God had dealt with our children in mercy and had drawn them to himself. They had already accepted Christ, and thus we could not only suffer but even die in peace. The children know God; the children are saved!

Yet now our home was empty and silent, the home that had once been cheerful and full of people, where sometimes we didn't get to bed until one or two o'clock in the morning because we would talk and sing and cry and rejoice together. Our daughter Lilia remained there alone in her grief. Sometimes it was very cold in the winter; but at night she slept in an unheated room.

At this point I have to mention that there was a period in the camp when I became bitter toward the Lord for allowing the arrest of my wife, who was so weak and ill. For about two days my heart was very dark and troubled. But then I came to my senses, prayed, and cried out to the Lord, "Please forgive me for thinking that I love her more than you do. I didn't die for her on Golgotha, Lord; *you* did. So do forgive me. I repent before you in dust and ashes." And the Lord answered my prayer. Even though I was grieved about my wife's imprisonment, I never again fell into such despair, for I knew how much God loved her. Whatever God gives us we must accept from his hands.

When I finished my term, I went home, got my children, and immediately went straight to the camp where my wife was being held. Although I had not seen her for a year and a half and asked for a short visit, the woman in charge refused. Then I asked the warden to let us see each other for just five minutes, so that my wife, seeing that I was now free and had come home, might be encouraged a little. The warden started shouting that everything was all my fault, that I had ruined my wife and my children, and that I should get out of there immediately so that Ulyana would not have to see my face. I listened to all of this calmly and then politely asked her to grant us a few minutes together. Finally she looked at my wife's file and saw that we were soon due for a long visit of three days.

"All right, you're due a visit, but not today. Come back on July twentieth. Now just get out of here!"

Since I was on a year's probation after my release, I had to go to the police station to get their permission for the visit. There I was assigned a specific route to travel and an itinerary. On July 20, the children and I packed some food and headed for the camp. The KGB was already there. My children recognized them from the trial. Obviously the police had informed them and had given them my itinerary. We saw them talking to one of the guards, and when we were brought in for a search, this guard went through all our bags very carefully, even opening envelopes and unwrapping chocolate bars. They were so afraid that we would try to take some literature in that they opened absolutely everything.

We were taken into the visiting room. When my wife was brought in we were shocked at her appearance. I did not think a person could get so thin, even in camp. The last time I had seen her was a year and a half before, when she came to visit me at my camp. At that time she had weighed 176 pounds and had been pretty solid. Now she was down to 88 pounds, and her arms and legs were like sticks. She was very weak and even got tired just talking, but her spirit was so cheerful and strong! We had brought a lot of food to give her some strength, but how much help can you give in two days? We hugged and cried and knelt together to thank God for the way he was leading us and for his constant presence and care.

During our visit I cooked some good food for Ulyana to give her some strength. She had not been able to eat the camp food. Anyone who has been in camp knows how bad the food is. They make gruel and soup out of nasty, greasy, half-rotten ingredients, and even a man who is completely healthy can barely stomach it. A sick person cannot take it at all. My wife was constantly violently sick to her stomach. We had petitioned the camp officials many times, asking that she be granted invalid status and thus allowed a special diet. The camp doctors informed us that they *had* granted her special status, but the KGB intervened each time and had it revoked.

We also observed the Lord's Supper together during our visit. It was a special moment for all of us, remembering the Lord's suffering and death. Our two days together passed very quickly. As we parted, Ulyana comforted and encouraged us. She said not to worry, that the Lord would preserve us all.

Two months later we were allowed another short visit with Ulyana. We arrived at the camp for our visit at 10:00 A.M., but we were not allowed to see her until 1:30 P.M. because they were making special preparations in the visiting room. The window that separated us from her was whitewashed on both sides so that we could barely see each other. The window where the monitor sits was covered with a screen so that we could not see who was there. Although other visiting rooms were empty, they would not let us move to one. Ulyana looked just as thin as before, but now she had to hold on to the walls as she walked.

After our visit my wife was put in the hospital and pumped full of fluids. But before long she was sent back to the camp again. She still has not been granted invalid status.

I am convinced that our persecutors have kept my wife imprisoned because she is a member of the Council of Prisoners' Relatives. The authorities told several of our

Despite the hardship of constant harassment by the authorities, Stepan Germaniuk continues to preach.

friends in the church that she could have been released earlier if it were not for her part in this ministry. For example, a preacher from the Crimea, Pyotr Shokha, was summoned for a "talk" with the KGB, and at one point he asked them, "Why are you keeping Germaniuk? Why don't you let her go?"

"We would have let her go a long time ago," they answered, "but she's a member of the CPR."

But praise God, I can rejoice in this because I see in the Scriptures a parallel in the situation with Saul and David. Nowhere does the Holy Spirit record that David feared Saul. It was Saul who was afraid of David. Saul was the ruler, and he persecuted David. But David was not afraid, for God was with him. Praise God, the situation is the same in our days. And since the Lord is with us, we know that victory is sure.

Postscript: Ulyana Germaniuk's condition continued to deteriorate until she was unexpectedly released on

March 25, 1987. She was able to attend the wedding of her daughter Lilia to Ivan Khorev in May of that year. However, on July 3, Ulyana Germaniuk died of stomach cancer. The funeral took place two days later, with fellow Christians from many cities attending and testifying of her faithfulness to God.

11

Zinaida Vilchinskaya
Prisoner Grandma

Before my arrest, I had a feeling that I would have to walk the path of sorrow, to go to prison. And I often checked up on myself. As I lived at home, warmly dressed and not hungry, I would ask myself, "What if a police car suddenly pulled up and they came with a warrant for my arrest and said, 'Get your things together'—would my heart fear?" I asked the Lord to give me the strength to prepare myself, and the Lord truly prepared me. Nothing in my house preoccupied me; I was ready to leave it all for the Lord. I knew that I

Zinaida Vilchinskaya was a 54-year-old grandmother when arrested on a train in May 1986 while carrying Christian literature. A member of the Council of Prisoners' Relatives, she was sentenced to two years of labor camp. Because of poor health and an outcry from Christians in the West, authorities released Mrs. Vilchinskaya in June 1987, eleven months early. Her husband, Vladimir, has spent six years in prison because of his ministry in the independent Baptist church in Brest. The Vilchinskayas have four children. Their daughter Galina has served two terms in camps because of her work with children.

could leave home and not look back as did Lot's wife. Then, when I was arrested, the Lord gave me strength.

When the police first took me to the police station, I was put in a very cold cell with bare iron bunks. The guards took my scarf and my coat, and I lay on the bunk in just a dress. I was shivering, and I started to pray. When my cellmate saw me pray, she, too, got on her knees and said, "Oh, I can't stand it. I'm freezing, too." She started to cry softly.

"Lord," I prayed, "if you want me to be frozen here, may your will be done; just enable me to endure this with love, submission, and meekness. But you can help me. You can even take me out of here if that's your will."

I lay back down and felt such warmth. I told the other woman, "Here, let me put my arm around you, and you'll get warmer." We warmed up together. Later, when they transferred us to different cells, she told everyone in hers, "God warmed up Aunt Zhenya [as they called me] in our cell, and she warmed me up." Even the guards smiled at me because this story was going all around. My former cellmate told everybody about it, and it was quite a testimony.

When the guards were transferring me and this other woman to the prison, I got my things together and waited quietly in the corridor. A guard grabbed my arms, and said, "Put your hands out." He held a pair of handcuffs. I just stood there, quietly looking at him. He repeated the order. Then he took my arm and cuffed me to the other woman. "Don't move, or it will tighten on your hand," he warned.

I put my arm down. "Do you have the right to put me in handcuffs?"

"What do you mean?"

"I'm a woman. What's more, I'm old, old enough to be

your mother. Could you handcuff your mother? You said to collect my things and come out, and I did. I'll go wherever you take me. I wasn't resisting, but you put these handcuffs on me. You don't have the right!"

"We have the right. That's the order, and that's what we'll do," the guard insisted.

"The whole world is going to find out about this. When my friends find out, don't accuse us of slandering the Soviet system. What you're doing is illegal."

The warden heard about what I had said. He came and told the guard to take the cuffs off me. "Hush, hush," he said. "We're taking them off already." They didn't try to handcuff me again.

Next they took me to an awful, damp, dark, bare prison cell. I entered the cell, greeted everyone, and said that I had been imprisoned because I am a Christian. I knelt—they made a little room for me—and I prayed. They listened closely. I also prayed for them, that the Lord would open the eyes of their spirits, that they might see. Terrible people were there, but this prayer touched their hearts and softened them. One even had tears because she was Orthodox and believed a little. Later she asked me many questions.

The conditions there were terrible. My mattress was damp. Everything was cement. I could not even put my feet down from the bed because the floor was so cold. But I rejoiced anyway, thanking the Lord for all these hardships. I reflected on how hard it was for Christ to suffer for our sins for our salvation. For me it was easy in comparison.

I was locked in the punishment cell twice in that prison, the first time for more than half a day. Everyone in my cell was taken there because a few prisoners had caused trouble. The second time was also for the crime of others. The guards knew that I was innocent and even said, "We know you haven't done anything." But all the same they put me in the punishment cell. Imprisoned in this cell, I thought about my dear friends who have had to spend fifteen to thirty days there. What a horrible place! The cell is unheated. The cement walls are rough, barbed, so that you will not lean against them. You can sit only on the cold, wet, cement floor. I looked at it all very carefully and was praying the whole time, thinking that maybe right now one of my friends was also locked in a punishment cell, and I asked the Lord to strengthen that person.

The Lord alone can preserve our friends and keep them from murmuring. In hard circumstances only the heart that is completely given to the Lord can keep from complaining. When unbelievers are imprisoned, they are full of despair and cursing. But praise the Lord that he gives his people enough strength to bear these griefs.

My own heart was such that I quickly forgave everyone, and I always tried to not allow a grudge against anyone into my heart. I prayed for them all.

The investigator asked me many questions, starting with the whereabouts of Gennady Kryuchkov. He already knew all about our brotherhood and talked about Georgi Vins. On the day of my arrest, I had told the investigator that I would be praying for him and his family, that they would come to know the joy of the Lord. He even said, "Okay, go ahead and pray."

The next year was the happiest time of my life. Every day I thanked God that he had sent me there to be a witness. I had many opportunities to speak to prisoners and guards. Many prisoners, seeing my faith, said, "Truly God is with her." Sometimes they even argued about me and my faith. I once heard one prisoner say to another,

"See how Christ helps her. See how happy she is, how easy it is for her. See how Christ works in her heart." I thanked the Lord because he truly did work in my heart. I never worried about what questions they would ask me. I had only one desire: to bear witness about the Lord and about the people of God. Many people in our country know believers only from slander campaigns in newspapers and radio. But during our talks the administrators acknowledged the truth. Some believed it right away, and others later.

One schoolteacher in prison had a high opinion of herself. When she learned that I was in prison for my faith in God, she tried to persuade me to change my beliefs. "Why do you put up with this?" she asked. "There is no God. You're going through this for nothing."

But, after being in the cell awhile, she changed her mind. She began to say, "Christ really does help Aunt Zhenya. See how powerful her Christ is! She wouldn't be able to survive here if it weren't for Christ."

A drug addict in my cell was assigned to "unwind" me, to get information out of me. But later she repented. "Forgive me for doing evil to you," she said, hugging me.

I forgave her and said, "May the Lord forgive you."

"When I leave here, I'll leave this business. I won't do it anymore."

I told her to seek God's people, and she promised that she would try to go to a worship service.

Then there were chances to witness at the trial. As I rode back and forth in the van, I had many talks with the young soldiers escorting me. "We never met people who believe in God as you do," they would say. "Surely your God is an amazing God. He really helps you."

One young soldier asked very serious questions. I told him we believe in the living God who can raise the dead, who helps us, who is always with us. The first day he was confused, but during the following days he constantly asked me questions. Before the trial he stayed nearby, still asking questions.

These people paid particular attention to me because I was really sick before and during the trial. "You're so sick and so joyful at the same time. It's truly only your God who holds you up," one said to me.

During the recesses of the trial, other lawyers came to talk. Although I had requested not to have a lawyer, the court forced me to have one, and talk about me spread to these others. "You didn't want us, but now you've told us so much about God," they said. "We're glad that we met you and learned so much about God from you." I, too, was happy about meeting these people and prayed for them.

After the trial, court workers also came to talk. The Lord gave me such wisdom that now it is hard even to tell what I experienced at that time of joy and difficulty. The Lord testified through me, and these people were amazed at the answers to their questions.

During the journey to camp, I witnessed in the transport prisons. In the Voronezh prison I met a woman who was going to exile in Khabarovsk and had already suffered much. After we became friends and prayed together, she took the news about Christ to her heart. She rejoiced, thanked God, and then thanked me.

"Don't thank me," I said. "The Lord led me here so that I could witness to you. If I weren't here, who would tell you?"

"Yes, that's right. I came here in order to meet you," she agreed.

The Lord gave a special blessing when I was put on a

regular passenger train. Realizing that Christians are special people, the guards moved me to a separate car so that I would not be close to the passengers. After that I had good conversations with the guards.

When I arrived at my camp, the administration summoned me and warned me to stop all talk about God.

"I'm a Christian," I replied. "I can't be silent. That's the reason God sent me here: to tell people about Jesus Christ." Despite the officials' protests, the Lord gave me the strength to witness to them.

The head of my work brigade turned out to be a cruel woman. She spoke to the prisoners only with fists and shouts. Everyone in the camp was afraid of her. Right in the beginning she summoned me and warned that I would be punished if I talked to anyone about God.

"I forbid you. And you will write no letters containing Bible verses," she said, adding that she had been given the job of re-educating me. It looked as if things were going to be bad for me there. But, with time, the Lord softened her heart toward me. Twice I saw tears in her eyes, and once she cried.

At first our conversations were frequent. I would listen to everything calmly, smile, and say, "Okay, fine." She zealously tried to turn me against God. Then, when she was powerless against my testimony, she brought in a captain to talk to me. This man was familiar with believers. He asked me questions about the CEBC and told me that the official in charge of religious cults filled him in on everything.

The administrators had also met with the religion official and learned about the CEBC. I was thankful to the Lord that they had this meeting because afterward the camp administration had a better attitude toward me.

After being assured that I really was from the CEBC group, the religion official told the administrators why we do not observe the *1929 Legislation on Religious Cults.* And they actually understood that it is not right to try to please both God and man. They agreed with me!

After my discussion with the captain, the leader of my brigade became even more pleased with me. Our conversations became much softer, but for a while she started to get upset if I said something about God. She yelled: "I forbid you! Don't say that. You've never seen him—there is no God."

"You can get mad at me if you want to," I replied, "but I can't do anything without the Lord. I'm always talking to him." In time it became a balm for her heart for me to quote the Word of God. When I talked to her about God, she would say, "May the Lord reward you."

I was not in the camp long before I started receiving mail. The first letter was from our youth group in Brest, and then individual families began to write. Of course, they were the first to find out my address; then friends in other cities learned of it, too. Soon a great stream of letters for me started to arrive at the camp. I received letters from the Ukraine—from Rovno, Zdolbunovo, Kivertsy, Kovel. It is impossible to list all the places mail came from—even distant places like Yakutia.

This mail was a great testimony. The letters witnessed about the Lord and spoke of his love. The administrators gave me whole packets of letters and said, "We've already checked them." They completely changed their views toward believers and toward the Lord. They became less cruel and more tolerant.

I got a lot of letters from children, and these were especially precious to me. I remember some children in

Leningrad who signed birthday cards and holiday messages. I tried to answer them all. Children in Valga wrote, too. The administration would summon me and ask, "Who are these children?"

"Oh, I have many children. These are God's children."

"But these kids are writing you."

"Of course," I said, "it's for their sake that I'm here. One of the accusations against me was violating the legislation that forbids us to raise children as Christians. That's why I'm imprisoned, and that's why the children write me."

So children wrote, and old women wrote, some who were barely able to write, and I tried to answer them and encourage them. It was very special when the children would send pictures. They would send pictures of flowers and say, "Here are flowers for you." For Easter they drew crosses, a sunrise, or resurrection pictures. The officer would summon me, look at the cards and say, "Oh, how lovely! What a good job these children did." So I received a great deal of encouragement from children.

Then a large number of letters started to come from abroad. Twice I was summoned and in my presence the officers opened the letters and read them. At first they were very strict about foreign letters, saying things like: "You said you don't have any connection with people outside the borders, but look at this. We're getting showered with letters from abroad."

I told them that Christians are joined by the love of Jesus Christ. "Everywhere—in every corner of the earth—we have friends, our relatives by the blood of Jesus Christ."

Before they had even opened the letters, I said, "If these were written by God's children, I can tell you with certainty that they will express only love and compassion for perishing sinners."

The officers came to realize the truth of my words. When they opened them, they read cards like the one that said, "Dear camp warden, I ask you sincerely to give this card to my sister in Christ, Zinaida Vilchinskaya." Further on, the card said, "We're praying for you. Every day when our family sits down to eat, we remember you. We ask the Lord to strengthen you and send you what you need for each day. We pray that the camp administration will be good to you."

The officer read this to me. "Yes, the love among you is very great," he commented. "No one else can do this. No other people have such friendship as there is among you." The administrators were really amazed. When they summoned me the second time, they opened them faster, read them all personally, and gave me the ones written in Russian to read.

Prayers and cards from abroad are a great support to the people of God, a balm to the soul. I took each card and letter with trembling. First I would pray and thank the Lord for the lovingkindness of my dear friends who wrote. Then, as I read, my heart would rejoice and be encouraged. I received new strength. How precious to receive verses, because in that camp we were deprived of everything, forbidden to even talk about God—and here I was, receiving wonderful verses from the Book of Life.

Then I received a package from Denmark. The whole camp heard about it. The administrators summoned me and said that they could not give it to me. I said, "Do what you want, but they sent it to me." They knew that they had no right to send it back without giving a reason for returning it. Then they said, "We'll send it to your husband."

"Okay, if I'm not allowed to have it, send it to him," I said. Instead they held on to it and gave it to me on the day of my release.

I soon discovered that even fasting is forbidden in camp. Not going to the mess hall is a violation of regime. Whether you want to or not, you have to go. The first time I fasted, I told a guard, "I'm fasting, I'm not going."

When she warned me that it was required that I go, I said, "Okay, I'll go. I'll just sit."

"You do what you like, but you have to be there."

Everyone was surprised when I did not eat. "How can you do that?" they asked.

"I'm in fellowship with the Lord," I said. "It's a special day of prayer."

The guard who had warned me to go to the meal asked, "Please pray for me, too." Many others asked me questions and requested prayer. On such days you really feel that the people of God are supporting you in prayer.

Finally, after a long separation of eight months, the administration permitted a two-day visit with my relatives. When the guards brought them in for a search, my little grandson saw me in the corridor. He smiled and came running to hug me, but a guard held him back. They put me in one room and my family in another. But this little three-year-old came out of his room, saw where they took me, and with tears, he took a piece of candy, opened the door, and said, "Grandma!" He tried to give me the candy.

The guard grabbed his arm. "Who let you in here? It's forbidden."

I kissed him on the head and told him to go back to the rest of them, and he slipped me the piece of candy. It was awkward for the guard, so she said, "Go ahead and take the candy." She took him by the arm and led him out crying. After the others were searched, I was allowed into their room.

Our meeting was very touching. I was sick: my kidneys hurt, I couldn't sleep at night, and I couldn't raise my arms or get undressed without help. My family said that I had really changed. First of all we prayed, thanking the Lord for the wonderful meeting he had granted us here on earth.

My family brought greetings from all our dear friends who were praying and supporting us. I was encouraged by this and grateful to the Lord. Of course, when they left, my relatives did not remain silent about my physical condition. They told our friends, and people started writing on my behalf. When the first telegrams came to the camp, the authorities summoned me and said, "Inform them that we've transferred you to another job so they'll quit writing and bothering us."

I can testify from my own experience how much the petitions of fellow believers helped me when I was in a desperate situation in the prison camp. Some Christians today say it is wrong to petition government authorities on behalf of suffering prisoners, that we should appeal only to the Lord. But the Lord is acting on this earth through people. Look at Esther and Mordecai and what they did in the day of grave trouble for God's people. The Lord used them to petition before the king on behalf of the Jews who were condemned, and he greatly blessed their efforts. God wants us to do the same today. He doesn't want us to remain silent, but rather, through our prayers and petitions, to help the prisoners who have been condemned to destruction by the enemies of the church.

I can testify to this even in little details in my life. For example, when I was working in the snow in ankle boots,

I never could dry them out, and I was always wet and sick. My family brought me good boots, but the administration refused to let me have them. But when the Christians petitioned about the boots, the administration gave permission. When the package with the boots came, they were running around the camp looking for me. "There's a package for you; please come and get it."

Afterward, if I was drying my new boots, the officers would ask, "Why aren't you wearing your boots?"

"I'm drying them."

"Well, wear them. Just tell your friends so they won't write anymore."

The administration made all kinds of concessions. When I was transferred to the carpentry section, they asked, "Is the work here too hard for you? Are you satisfied with your work? Your friends are writing." Other prisoners would be fainting, and no one paid any attention to them, but the Lord through his people so inclined the hearts of the authorities that they were even asking me such questions as "Is it too hard for you? Do you need to be moved to another job?" Praise God for his mercy and for the wonderful prayers and petitions of his people.

The Lord manifested his mercy to me in other ways as well. For example, in the barracks you cannot pray. From dawn to dusk the barracks are filled with people, noise, and obscene language. During the whole day there is hardly ever a time when no one is there. But the Lord gave me a place at work to dwell with him: "Mount Tabor," as I called it. I went to work at seven, and no one else got there until around eight. I would kneel and pour out my heart before the Lord and find amazing help. I was able to read there, too. I took my letters to work with me because there was no opportunity in the barracks. The officials do frequent searches and collect letters. You can keep a few, but more than that they force you to destroy. So I kept my letters with me at work, rereading them often. My friends wrote out songs, and I would sing. Every morning I tried to spend time on Mount Tabor, feeding my soul before I continued my earthly, physical labor.

In the camp yard I tried to be in constant fellowship with the Lord, and my soul was in such delight that with my twig broom in hand I barely saw the prisoners sitting around. I swept and I sang. The other women were surprised. "Why are you always singing? What are you so happy about?" they asked.

They soon learned that I am a believer and that this old Christian grandma sings for and about the Lord. My favorite hymn was "You Know the Path, Though I Do Not Know It." I didn't remember all the words of the song, but I repeated it over and over, from the time I got up until I went to bed at night. That song explains why I always had peace in my heart—the Lord knows my path.

Coming back to the barracks after work, the Lord granted me such strength that I was defended against all these things surrounding me. I never even felt the vile language. At times I woke up wondering, *Am I still here, or has the Rapture come and taken me from the earth?* But then I looked around and saw all the prisoners and knew I was still in camp.

In my barracks and in my work brigade were a lot of older women, some quite elderly. We had invalids and pensioners. The old women were primarily murderers, tormented by sin. Many had been abandoned. Nobody wrote to them. Prisoners and authorities alike despised them. They were bitter against everyone, but I asked the Lord to give me the opportunity to approach these calloused souls with stone hearts.

One elderly woman who worked beside me had been imprisoned for seven years, and she knew nothing but swearing and coarseness. In the beginning I witnessed to her by kindness. I tried to be gentle and to speak kind words. This touched her heart.

"You're a living soul," I told her. "You should pray and ask God to forgive you."

"How can I pray when I've committed such a terrible crime? God doesn't hear me anymore. God doesn't need me. Nobody needs me."

"The Lord told the thief on the cross, 'Today you will be with me in paradise,' and if you also receive him, he'll receive you." She took in all this with such emotion that I said to her, "Pray."

"But how do I pray?" she wondered.

"Just as a child would talk to a father, that's how you should ask for forgiveness."

I saw her go to a corner of the yard, cross herself, and pray. I approached her, talked with her, and from then on she drew close to me.

The others at work were curious to learn why I was there. Their fondness for me was evident when an official came through and made fun of me for being a believer. "You don't know what you're saying. Stop it," my co-workers forbade him and defended me. After this he treated me with respect. Thus the Lord gave me opportunities to witness to my fellow workers.

The holidays gave me special opportunities to share my faith. On Christmas morning I got up and with a joyful smile gave holiday greetings to my nearest neighbor, then to another. They got sheepish smiles on their faces, and then they remembered. "Oh, that's right. It's Christmas."

"But what *is* Christmas?" I asked the prisoners. "Do

you know what it means?" Some knew, but the majority
did not. Some gave answers such as "Yes, that's when
God was born," and had their own ideas about that.

Others asked, "When and how was he born? Why did
Jesus Christ come to earth?" The whole day was filled
with such conversations.

The next day at work I gave holiday greetings to my
co-workers. They asked me all about Christmas. "How
do you celebrate?" the old women asked. I explained how
the people of God celebrate this special day, but the main
desire of my heart was to tell about Christ's birth, about
his wondrous coming into this world.

Then in April came Easter. At that time I was in the
infirmary, but early Easter morning I greeted my neighbor with the traditional greeting: "Christ is risen!"

"He is risen indeed!" she answered.

Then the nurse came and said good morning.

"Christ is risen!" I said, smiling. She, too, gave the
joyful response. I thanked God, glad that people can be
just barely alive and still see the truth and answer this
wondrous greeting.

That day several prisoners from my work brigade came
to see me. First two women came. One was very near to
the Lord. We had had many conversations, and she had
read many of my letters. Then came a very cruel woman
who worked next to me on the job. I never thought that
she would visit me. Later three young girls came, and to
my surprise they smiled and said, "Christ is risen!" I had
talked to them a lot about the Lord. They were very
interested and were close to me. Then others came also,
so the Lord comforted me even through these prisoners.
Nobody from the other brigades had any visitors, but
many people came to see me on the day of our Lord Jesus
Christ's resurrection. And the most special thing was

that they came and greeted me with the words "Christ is risen!"

The next day the head doctor was there. Seeing him, I called out, "Christ is risen!" He looked at me and said, "Vilchinskaya, he is risen indeed!" I was really pleased. During the holiday I met no one among the medical staff or prisoners who did not respond to my greetings. Some didn't know how to answer and just repeated the same words, "Christ is risen," so then I would say, "He is risen indeed!"

I received many Easter greeting cards, and gave them to others in my ward to read. What a testimony! They were delighted as they read one after another.

One woman in the infirmary read all my letters and cards and came to the Lord. After we were discharged, we tried to have some kind of fellowship, even though it was strictly forbidden to interact with prisoners from other brigades. Through the fence or in passing, we tried to say a word of encouragement to one another. She asked many questions about the Lord and his love. This soul remained close to the Lord, and I was very happy that I had met her.

It was through his people that the Lord brought about the miracle of my release. At the beginning of March the public prosecutor had come with the order, summoned me to the office, and suggested very subtly that here was an opportunity to go home.

"Just write that you'll no longer be involved in your criminal activity," he said.

"I didn't commit any crime and can't write that I did."

"You can believe what you want, but write a statement," the officials tried to persuade me. One of the officers even hinted, "Yes, you can believe, and you can continue your work—only write."

"No, I can't be a hypocrite. If I'm to continue my work, that means I can't write," I insisted.

They tried to convince me that there are many people who believe in God and go along with them.

"Perhaps," I agreed. "Even the demons believe and tremble before God, but look what they do. And there are many people who believe in God but aren't faithful to him. But the Lord doesn't want only our dead belief; he wants faithfulness. I want to be true to him to the end."

I turned to the prosecutor. "You're too late," I said. "I once promised the Lord to serve him with a good conscience, and I cannot betray him to my death. I won't write anything."

"So you don't want to go home. You can keep clearing snow," he said in a gruff tone.

I stood, asked permission to leave, wished them that the Lord would give them the strength to see his beauty and to know the truth, then left.

After this visit from the public prosecutor, I became well known among both the prisoners and the authorities. I had opportunities to speak to many people about the Lord and to explain why I did not accept the pardon. The leaders from all the brigades came to me, asking, "Why don't you want to go home? What's your motive in staying here?"

I was even summoned by almost the top man in the camp, the head of the operative division. "Why don't you want to go home? It was stupid of you to reject the pardon of our government. It comes to you as a concession, and you have the opportunity to go. It's still not too late to write it."

I told him why I had not accepted the pardon. He listened well, and we had such a good talk. In the end he told me, "You've done the right thing, to continue in such a spirit. You'll be freed this year because there will be a big amnesty. You'll be released because of your age."

I attribute this conversation to the Lord, because the Lord is stronger than all to encourage and reinforce our strength. Through this man's lips, the Lord said to me, "Don't worry. Have patience. A little while longer, and you will go home. Even though it is hard for you, be strong."

I thanked the man and left. Then I thanked the Lord for these words. Not because I would be home, but because these people, the rulers of this world, saw the power and truth of God. And they encouraged me. Praise the Lord.

I was summoned two more times in connection with the pardon. The last offer came just two weeks before the amnesty. The officers summoned me to read me letters from friends in other countries, saying, "See how they're asking on your behalf? But we can't let you go. We would be glad to let you go, but we can't. Write a statement, and you can leave." So I also had the opportunity to tell the warden about the truth of God. He agreed with me completely. "You're right," he said, "but that means we'll have to keep you here to the end."

My brigade leader also tried to prepare me for a conditional early release, but I told her that her efforts were in vain. "I would have to acknowledge myself guilty and repent," I said. "But I didn't commit any crime, can't acknowledge myself guilty, and can't repent, so please don't do this." Then she offered to do all the explaining for me.

"If you're going to say that maybe I'll change my views," I continued, "I don't want you to. I don't want any untruth in my life, through my own lips or those of others."

The camp authorities did not even bother to call me up before the commission—they knew it was no use.

Then, before the amnesty, I had to go to the brigade leader's office after work. I was really tired and, sitting in the hallway outside the door, I was in such fellowship with God that I noticed nothing around me. I was sitting there when here came the brigade leader down the hall. According to our camp's strict rules, when she approaches, prisoners are supposed to stand up. It is a violation of regime if you are not standing, but I kept sitting because I didn't notice her.

The brigade leader opened the office, and I quickly stood, saying, "Excuse me; I was deep in thought and didn't notice you."

"It's okay; don't worry. Come on in," she smiled.

"Soon there will be an amnesty," she said. "You might be able to leave. How's your health? How's the work?" She had read my letters carefully, and I believe that through them the Lord had said much to the soul of this cruel woman. She always asked me about the letters and poems. She questioned me so sincerely and toward the end even rejoiced that some of my friends had returned home from prison camps. "Here your friends write that some are being released. Maybe soon you'll go, too."

"You're so kind to me," I said. "The Lord won't forsake you. I have one desire in my heart—that you would come to know his joy."

"I see that you have joy, but you're an unusual woman. You've made a great impression on me." She was really crying. She put her head down. "Oh, Vilchinskaya, you've touched my heart so—I can't talk." She wiped her tears and could not control herself.

"I wish you only good," I said. "Understand that I

don't hold any ill will for you or your family. I really want you to have the joy of salvation."

I saw that she was upset. I got up, stood for a while, then said, "May I go?"

"Go." She wiped her tears and hid them, but that scene remains in my mind. After that I prayed even more for her, asking the Lord to open her eyes. Later, when this woman heard the news of my imminent release, she rejoiced. Coming to me at work, she cried out, "You're going home!"

"Yes," I said, "I'm going home, but you'll stay here, and maybe we'll never meet again on earth."

"Mountains don't move, but people meet. We might meet again."

"If you ever want to meet believers, there are some even here in Gomel. You can meet them." I wished her joy and peace from the Lord. She cried.

My release came about in an unexpected way. The warden of the camp came to the guard house and said to me, "We're very glad that we met you and had all these conversations with you. We're very happy about your release. Maybe you could have left earlier with the first amnesty, but now Moscow has freed you."

I asked him on what grounds I was to be released.

"On orders from Moscow," he replied, "from the Supreme Soviet."

"But I didn't request a pardon."

"Your believers wrote petitions, and because of all their requests to the Supreme Soviet, you're being released." The warden said he hoped I would never end up there again.

"You know that I'm not here for committing a crime. You know that it was for God's work," I reminded him.

Zinaida
Vilchinskaya has
had many
opportunities to
share her prison
experiences at
church meet-
ings.

Christians in Russia express their love with flowers. Christians in the West express their love with letters. Mr. and Mrs. Vilchinsky are enjoying both, glad to be reunited and home again.

"Just don't come back."

I said good-bye to everyone at the morning search and wished them all the best of God's blessings and that they might come to know the Lord. I knew that I was going home, that there was nothing to fear. They were all crying. One woman fell on my neck, saying, "What will I do without you?"

I also saw the woman who had come to Christ in the infirmary. She was on the other side of a fence, walking by behind an office. I waved and said, "I'm going home." She ran to the fence.

"You're going home? What about me? What will I do without you?"

"You'll be here for a while yet," I said quietly. "May the Lord help you to leave this place." She started to cry. We waved and parted.

The administration saw me off very kindly. The warden looked at me and said, "Vilchinskaya, you're such a respectable woman, but you're dressed so badly. You should change, but we see that you don't have any clothes in the locker."

"That's right."

"But you must change."

"I look fine," I assured him.

"Will anyone meet you?"

"No one will meet me because no one knows."

"And if they knew, would they meet you?"

"Absolutely, they would come right here."

"Well, will they meet you at home?"

"If they find out, they will. But if they don't know, they won't."

"Do you know anyone in Gomel?" the warden persisted.

"Yes, I have some brothers and sisters in Christ."

"Well, the head of your brigade will take you to the store. We'll give you some help, and she'll buy you a dress so that you can change."

I thanked him for his thoughtfulness and for wanting to help but said I really needed nothing, that I could go to the store myself to buy clothing. "I have some money that my family sent, so if I must change, I will."

"No, she'll go with you, show you where the store is, and help you. You wait for her."

In the guard house they slowed down my release with their talking. But when they saw that it was already time to release me, they could keep me no longer. The warden told me I was free but said, "Vilchinskaya, I really ask you, please don't go yet. Wait for your brigade leader. She'll be right here."

"Since you ask me so sincerely," I said, "I'll wait." Actually, I wanted to see her again anyway.

I walked out the gate, raised my eyes, and thanked the Lord. Standing there, I could scarcely believe I was outside the camp. My heart was torn. Thinking back to just a few minutes before, in my mind's eye I once more saw those sobbing old women during our last moments together. They had wept and hugged me, especially the one old woman who was a murderer. She fell on my neck, sobbing, and it broke my heart. Not until the moment of my release did I realize how close she had drawn to me. My heart had been so touched that I had even prayed, "Lord, perhaps if but for the sake of this soul I could stay here a little longer. . . ."

As I stood there reflecting, I felt I still had not done everything I could, that perhaps I should stay in the camp, telling the officers and prisoners about the love of God. "If it's your will," I prayed, "open the gates, and I'll go back and tell them more." But I believe and know that apart from the will of God, not a hair falls from the head, and therefore that my release also was not contrary to God's will.

I saw my brigade leader coming. As we walked together, I looked back. "Why are you looking back?" she asked.

"I feel so sorry for those poor people."

"Of course you do, because that's the kind of heart you have. You care about everybody. But they're the kind that should never be let out."

With this remark, the Lord gave me another chance to tell about him. "It was for the sake of such people that the Lord came to earth. It's not the righteous who need to repent, but those forgotten ones, these sinners whom no one needs. He came to save their souls. He poured out his blood to save sinners." She listened quietly.

Soon we reached the store. The brigade leader was in a military uniform, I in a ragged prison dress. I chose a dress and put it on. After paying, the brigade leader shook my hand. "I'm so glad I met you. You've left a good mark in my heart. I won't forget you." And so we parted.

I walked the streets of Gomel, looked at all the goods being sold, and bought myself a meat pastry. However, remembering those poor women in the camp, I couldn't even eat it. Even though I had eaten only a little bread that morning, I just couldn't. The Lord showed me once again that if he sends us into bonds, we should go joyfully to witness about Christ.

After I got my train ticket, I called home. My children had already heard about my release. I also found out that my daughter Galina would be there that night. The camp administration had granted me a visit with my family on the eighteenth and nineteenth, and she was already on her way. I was so cheered up to talk to them on the phone.

In the meantime my heart longed for the people of God. I wanted to find a Christian and pour out my gratitude to God. I had two addresses of believers in Gomel from letters I had received. I found the house of one woman, but she didn't recognize me. "You used to be rather heavy," she said. We prayed together, then I went to the other address. We had such a wonderful time of fellowship—so many tears, such joy, such comfort.

These friends accompanied me to the train station. Then friends in Kobrin met me on the way to Brest. My family in Brest had informed them that I was coming through, so they came looking for me. They started searching through all the train cars while I was wondering if I would see anyone I knew. Suddenly there they were! What joy there was on that train. We prayed, cried, and talked.

We arrived in Brest where we were met by other friends, but also by adversaries—the authorities. None of our friends had known which car I was in, but one sister overheard two KGB agents walking by, mentioning that Vilchinskaya would be in car number twelve. So all the Christians knew where to meet me. The meeting was very heart-touching. About thirty people were there— my children, grandchildren, and friends young and old. They took up the whole exitway. Everyone was filled with great joy.

When we got home more friends and neighbors were waiting for me. Some neighbors even cried, and one brought flowers. We prayed and sang outside. Just then the police drove up, watching us from their cars. But no one tried to stop us. Then we went into the house, and the friends stayed a long time. Later, when just my husband, children, and grandchildren remained, the children brought me the promise box to choose a verse. I got Proverbs 31:8–9: "Open thy mouth for the dumb in the cause of all such as are appointed to destruction. Open thy mouth, judge righteously, and plead the cause of the poor and needy."

The Lord spoke to me through this verse because for a long time I had been hindered in my ministry. I had always felt such sympathy for all the unfortunate ones, and when I was chosen for this ministry, I found my calling. I knew without a doubt that the Lord had done this, and my heart was very grateful to the Lord for this ministry. But, even before my arrest, some people, including relatives, were advising, "You should give yourself a break and stop this work. Others can do this ministry. Why must you?" I often had to be away from home for more than a week at a time, and there was Grandmother to look after, and my husband was not well, and many other difficulties.

"Lord," I had prayed, "even if my friends, brothers, and sisters are now saying, 'Don't go; someone else can do it,' You know the desire of my heart is to be true to you to my last breath. From my childhood it's been the desire of my heart to defend the poor and needy." Now, when the Lord again spoke to me through this verse, I asked my family, "What do you think about this? Who is speaking through this Scripture?"

"The Lord."

"And if the Lord says this, can I ignore it? Can I fail to obey him when he has shown me so many great mercies and led me—led all of us—by such a wondrous path? Can we ignore this call from the Lord?"

"No," my husband answered, "we must obey it."

Next I asked each of the children their opinion. "Tell me honestly: do you agree that I should take on this work again, and will you help me in this ministry?"

With tears in their eyes, all of them promised the Lord to serve him in this field with renewed strength. We prayed, "Here we are. Take us and put us where you want us. Not where we would like to be, but where you decide." I was so thankful to the Lord that our family was one in thought, in complete agreement, and this fulfilled the desire of my heart.

Now, in conclusion, I can say that the persecution of God's people is a blessing from the Lord. We receive this persecution with joy. When I was imprisoned, I often remembered how the apostles sang when they were in jail. In our days the world is surprised when God's children sit in prison and sing. Why do they sing? They sing because they are blessed by God. Those who are sent there go with the Lord.

Of course, my body was weak. I had moments of great sickness. But my spirit was so healthy that it mastered my body. When I was at the end of my strength, I would say, "Lord, you see how hard this is." And my spirit mastered the weakness of my flesh. I can say with assurance that these bonds, which the Lord sent me into, were an amazing blessing from him. I cannot explain the blessing of these griefs that he sent into my life, but the Lord wondrously led me through them.

12

Aleksei Kalyashin
Almost a Groom

T he day of my arrest, I set off for work as usual, but I had only one thought in my mind— preparations for the wedding. The authorities had often broken up worship services in our church, but I just didn't think they would arrest me then, not right before the wedding. Even as I began working, all my thoughts were on the wedding: what things to buy, where to buy them, and what still needed to be done.

Around noon two policemen entered the shop. I saw

Aleksei Kalyashin (b. 1955) was first arrested in September 1981, just one week before his wedding date. Three years later, when friends gathered at the camp gates in Nizhny Ingash on September 1, 1984, to welcome Kalyashin back to freedom, he was not there. Authorities had instead transferred him to Krasnoyarsk to face new "criminal" charges. On the basis of false and fabricated evidence, Aleksei was found guilty and sentenced to an additional two and a half years of imprisonment. He later married his fiancée in a civil ceremony at the camp in June 1985. Finally back in freedom, Aleksei was recently ordained into the ministry.

them but paid no special attention until they walked straight up to me, one of them on each side, and took hold of both my arms. I was surprised, but I didn't realize this was an arrest.

A man in civilian clothes carrying a briefcase pulled out a paper. "Are you Kalyashin, Aleksei Aleksandrovich?" he asked.

"Yes."

"You're under arrest!" he said and showed me the warrant. Only then did I finally realize what was happening. They put me in a car and drove me to the prison in Vladimir.

On the way I again thought about the wedding. Only now I was thinking of how it would have to be postponed for long years. I wondered how Nina, my sweetheart, would take the news of my arrest. I asked the Lord to help us bear having our hopes and plans wiped out. Then I remembered the Scripture verse on our wedding invitations, "Father, glorify thy name!" (John 12:28), and I asked the Lord to glorify his name even through this unexpected turn of events.

While the guards were leading me down the prison corridor, I imagined the cell, large and filled with dozens of people cursing and fighting. I was mentally gearing myself up for that moment, asking the Lord to help me. But when the guard opened the cell door, I saw a small room with only one old man sitting in it. We soon got acquainted, and I learned he had already been imprisoned for more than twenty years. I told him how I had been arrested for Christian activities. He had many questions, so we talked all evening about God and Christian faith.

After three days I was taken out for a meeting with my mother, who was anxious about my wedding plans.

"Mama," I said, "all this happened so suddenly—first

my arrest and soon a trial. Tell Nina I'm sorry, but she shouldn't feel obliged to wait three years for me. She's free from her promise. I won't be offended if she marries someone else. I'll understand." At that point our visit was cut off, and Mama was taken out.

The investigator strongly urged me to compromise. Using my wedding plans as a lure, he offered me freedom. In exchange he asked me to write a statement saying that the Bible does not contradict the *1929 Legislation on Religious Cults* and that I agree to abide by this legislation. He even offered to let me speak into a tape recorder instead of writing my statement.

The investigator always concluded our conversations with the reminder, "Aleksei, your wedding is scheduled for September nineteenth. You can be free by then. You're a young man. Why should you go to prison camp for three years instead of getting married? Think about it."

I told him I would never compromise my Christian convictions. I asked the Lord for help to stand firm in this struggle and to keep me faithful to him.

Before the trial I asked the investigator to permit a meeting with my fiancée. He agreed to fifteen minutes in his presence. With her first words Nina started to encourage me, but I felt obligated to say, "Nina, they're promising to sentence me to three years. We aren't talking about three days or three months. This is a long term. You shouldn't have to wait for me! I'm releasing you from your promise to marry me."

"Alex," she answered, "I love you, and I'll stand by my promise to be your wife for my whole life."

"Investigator Vladimir Vladimirovich offers to free me if I agree to say the Bible doesn't contradict the *1929*

Legislation on Religious Cults. How do you feel about this offer?"

Nina looked me straight in the eyes. "We can't even discuss the subject!"

I thanked the Lord for giving me a girlfriend who agreed with me on the most vital issues.

"Nina," I said, "the Lord will help us to walk this path of trials."

"Of course, Alex, Jesus won't forsake us. I'll be much in prayer for you."

Our meeting ended. I returned to the cell with gladness in my heart. I told my cellmate about the meeting with Nina and about how deeply we understood and loved each other.

At the trial, many believers gathered outside the building but were not permitted to enter. In fact, out of all my friends and family, only my mother was allowed to attend.

When I refused the atheist lawyer for the defense, the judge asked, "Just whom do you want as a defense lawyer?"

"I could entrust my defense only to a Christian lawyer who is familiar with the Bible's teachings and is able to understand the motives for my actions."

"There's no such lawyer in our whole country."

"In that case," I replied, "I don't object if the Christian lawyer comes from abroad." The judge rejected the request.

The trial lasted two days. The accusation against me was of leading the worship service in our church and thereby disrupting public order. The primary witnesses were members of the volunteer patrol and policemen who had broken up our meetings. Of course, other Christian witnesses and I explained that our peaceful services did not disturb public order at all.

When the judge withdrew to the conference room before pronouncing the sentence, I was led away to a room where the plainclothesman—a KGB major—wanted to question me.

"Aleksei, what's your opinon of Gennady Kryuchkov? Would you agree he's simply a vagrant preacher?"

"No!" I answered. "Pastor Kryuchkov is a minister of the gospel, selected by the church and respected by all believers. He's not a vagrant preacher."

He asked me many other questions, then picked up the telephone receiver, called the judge's conference room, and told him what sentence to give me. And, just as he had said, I got three years. I was told to get ready for transport.

"But we have a law saying prisoners are to be put in a camp near where they live," I said to the head officer. "Why am I being sent somewhere else?"

"Yes, you're right," he replied. "A law does say prisoners are usually to be sent to camps near their homes, but exceptions exist—maybe one in a thousand. And here you are—this is just such a rare incident."

During the transport the guards crammed about thirty of us into one train compartment. We received few meals. I passed through several prisons, but the most horrible conditions were in the Sverdlovsk prison. One hundred thirty of us were stuffed into a cell intended for thirty. We had nowhere to lie down, not even enough places to sit. So we all sat on the grimy floor on our sacks, awaiting the next stage of transport.

The first day there one man with a cruel face and long arms walked among the new arrivals, rummaging through each one's belongings. He took whatever he wanted, and no one dared to object.

When someone asked me what I was in for, I explained

that I am a Christian, imprisoned for preaching the gospel. All those who had previously met believers in other prisons reacted immediately. They offered me food and found a place on the bunks for me to rest. Then I was bombarded with questions the rest of my days in Sverdlovsk.

Finally the transport reached its destination, and I arrived at a camp situated in Siberia, in the Krasnoyarsky region. I had a Bible with me, since in prison I had written an application, requesting permission to have one. But in camp the guards snatched it away from me.

"I'd rather die than let you have a Bible in camp!" said the head of the operative division, Senior Lieutenant Danilchenko. "Over my dead body!"

Later I talked with the officers several times, asking for my Bible, but they answered, "Which article are you sentenced under? For religion? And you still want a Bible here? If you were in for murder or something else, maybe then we'd consider it. But to give a Bible to a religious fanatic—there won't be any of that!"

Right away I found another Christian in the camp— Sergei Bublik, convicted with a printing team from the Christian Publishing House. We had not known each other before, but I rejoiced that now I was no longer alone. We remained together for eight months.

The conditions in camp were oppressive. There was not much food, and even water had to be hauled in. The administration permitted us only a little water for washing, not enough for personal laundry.

Sergei helped me since he had already learned how to cope in camp. We spent time together after work, talking, praying, and sharing news from freedom. Other prisoners sometimes said, "How do you find so much to talk about? Don't you get sick of each other? After all, here in camp even when relatives or neighbors meet, they spend two or three evenings together, talk over everything, and that's the end of it."

We explained that the love of the Lord Jesus Christ and the blood he shed on the cross made us brothers. As for subjects for conversations, we could never run out because we talked about the Bible, the ways of the Lord, and how the Lord leads us. We also told them we had many mutual friends who sent us letters, which we shared with each other. So our friendship became a testimony of our brotherhood in Christ.

The amount of mail we received also astonished the other prisoners. Sergei normally received twenty letters a day and up to one hundred a day near holidays. During Christmas of 1983 I got more than three hundred letters and cards. Friends sometimes sent whole chapters from the Bible, Christian poems, and hymns. Sergei and I kept no secrets from each other. We always read our letters together, even those I received from Nina.

Before I arrived at the camp, Sergei had had great troubles with his correspondence. For four months the administration had not given him a single letter with Christian contents. His family found out and complained, and as a result his mail was restored.

I decided to send the public prosecutor of Krasnoyarsky region a complaint about my Bible being taken away. After some time he came to resolve the matter, and I was summoned for a discussion. He said I could have the Bible as long as I read it alone and did not give it to other prisoners. The prosecutor told Danilchenko, the operative division chief (the same officer who had told me he would rather die than give me the Bible), to step in. Then he asked him where my Bible was.

"In the safe," Danilchenko replied.

The prosecutor asked him to get the Bible and give it to me. Danilchenko had no choice but to submit. I returned to the barracks with my Bible!

Before Easter, Sergei and I decided to do something special for our prisoner friends. Our camp was famished, and the work was exhausting. Many people got sick from lack of vitamins and general emaciation. We began setting aside bread, jam, and margarine in order to have holiday treats. On the day of Christ's resurrection, we wished everyone a joyful holiday and then cut the bread, spread it with margarine and jam, and gave it to everyone who wanted some. Many men accepted this hospitality with tears in their eyes; they knew we had deprived ourselves in order to share with them.

Eight months after I had arrived in camp, I was suddenly told to get ready for transport. An officer told me I was being transferred on the KGB's orders.

Parting with Sergei was heartbreaking. We had lived through so much together. Having a brother in Christ beside me had been a great support. Now the unknown lay ahead. On parting, Sergei gave me a verse from Genesis 31:49: "The LORD watch between me and thee, when we are absent one from another."

I was moved out in October. Just a month before, I had had a visit from my family, and Mama had brought me some felt boots, a padded jacket, and a hat. The authorities had taken all these things, put them in storage, and given me a receipt, saying I could have everything in winter. But when I went to the head officer with the receipt before transport, he simply took the receipt away. So I was driven away to face winter in light clothing.

My new camp was situated in Nizhni Ingash. Life there was much harsher than in the first camp. The barracks were overcrowded, and although the bunks were stacked three high, many men ended up sleeping on the floor. In addition to a lot of bugs and lice, a contagious skin disease raged in the camp. My first time in the baths I was shocked that the majority of the prisoners had scabs covering their whole bodies. You got the impression that their bodies were rotting away. In my first camp a person in such a condition would have been immediately sent to the infirmary and given medical care. Here no one paid any attention.

I asked the Lord to preserve me from this excruciating disease, taking Psalm 91 as the basis for my prayer. And the Lord heard me—for all my years in that camp, I never got that infectious disease, even though the affliction and I lived in constant contact.

Procedures also differed from those in my first camp. For example, in the evenings after work and supper we were not permitted to walk back to the barracks. Instead we were held in a corridor until "lights out." There we would stand, packed into the prisoners' corridor, waiting several hours for bedtime.

At first I was lonely and depressed in the new camp. Then one evening when we were all packed into the corridor as usual, one prisoner suddenly asked, "Where are you from, buddy? And what are you convicted for? Which article?"

I told him, and he perked up.

"So you're a believer? There was another Christian here with us, Aleksander Nikitkov, freed not long ago. A good guy! So you're one of them?"

At this point he said something to the chief prisoner, who walked over and started asking me questions. We ended up having a conversation about God, and my spirit revived. I no longer felt forgotten and lonely. Once more the Lord had given me a ministry.

Soon other prisoners told me about KGB workers who had begun coming to the camp, conducting investigations and questioning prisoners who lived or worked with me. The KGB asked them to turn in written reports about me.

"Aleksei," said one man, "KGB officials have summoned me several times asking about you, and the last time they told me to find some violation against you so they can lock you up for fifteen days. I don't want to raise my hand against you! I can't do that! But they demanded. What should I do?"

But what could I advise him? "You decide yourself," I said. "It will be on your conscience."

After this conversation I constantly checked my belongings, looking under the mattress, in my pockets, everywhere. Someone could easily slip in a knife or something else forbidden and later "find" it. But that man never did anything against me. Later he confided how he had been coached to get more familiar with me, to ask questions about my past and my church, then to inform the KGB on everything.

Obviously the KGB were preparing a new term for me. They checked and re-checked all my mail, eventually finding fault with one letter to my mother. When an amnesty for prisoners was announced for the sixtieth anniversary of the USSR, Mama wrote that maybe I would return home under amnesty. I wrote back that we should not put our hope in the officials' humanity but in the grace of God. The KGB confiscated this letter and locked me up for fifteen days "for a letter of slanderous character against the Soviet government and social order."

As Christmas drew nearer, I received more than three hundred letters for the holidays. I rejoiced and thanked the Lord, but the other prisoners could hardly believe so many people cared about me. After returning to the barracks on Christmas Eve, about ten of us wanted to celebrate. One of them was from a Christian family. His mother and sister were members of the church, but he himself had lived a sinful life and ended up in this camp, where we met. This man became quite attached to me. The others, too, had become interested in Jesus Christ.

We had just gathered together when someone called me outside. There stood a prisoner who usually worked outside the camp and was brought back only at night. He pulled a packet out from under his jacket and handed it to me.

"What's this?" I asked. "Who's it from?"

"Do you know Daria?"

"Yes," I said. This Christian woman, who lived in the settlement by our camp, had already sent me warm footwear and underclothes several times. "When did you see her?"

"Just now. She's still standing over there, just outside the camp."

I was overwhelmed. This was Christmas Eve, when everyone rushes to be with loved ones or at a worship service. But to come to a camp late at night, in winter, in order to pass a bit of joy to an imprisoned brother in Christ—this was an astounding display of Christian love! Barely able to hold back my tears, I thanked the prisoner and took the packet into the barracks.

We unwrapped the packet together, finding chocolate and some pieces of candy. I divided the chocolate into ten portions. We each got only a tiny piece, but through this gift the Lord deeply touched the hearts of my friends. Our mood was joyful and festive. After I passed out slips of paper with Bible verses on Christ's birth, we concluded Christmas Eve by reading these verses together.

My term was approaching its end, but I felt storm clouds brewing over me. The preparation of materials against me for a new term intensified. Prisoners were summoned and questioned about me. The authorities were interested in my every move. After conversations with the KGB, prisoners started to ask me questions on subjects they were completely unfamiliar with. For example, they asked me about ministers in the Council of Evangelical Baptist Churches—where they lived and what each one's specific ministry included—and questions about internal church matters that are never discussed with strangers. KGB workers kept many prisoners for four or five hours at a time, demanding evidence against me. Sometimes the prisoners recounted these conversations to me.

I understood what all this was leading up to: I would not be freed at the end of my three-year term. This was heavy to bear. Nina and I had once again laid wedding plans, deciding to have a combined homecoming celebration and wedding. At that moment, when the threat of resentencing was so real, spiritual support was essential for me, so I wrote to Vladimir Ivanovich, the preacher who had led my family to the Lord. I asked him to support me in prayer, just as Aaron and Hur supported Moses in order to win the battle.

I still kept hoping for my scheduled release. And in my final days everything pretty much quieted down. Four days before my release date I received the checklist and began gathering the appropriate signatures, verifying I had returned all camp property. I also began to say farewell to everyone.

Two days before my release date an investigator came

to the barracks and asked, "Where's your night stand, Kalyashin? I have to look through your papers."

He started to make a search. I had little left. The other prisoners had asked me to leave them some mementos, especially the postcards, and I had already given away almost everything. But the investigator emptied my shelf. Later I was summoned to the office and told I was being charged with Article 190. There would be another trial, and I could get up to three years.

The guards took me to the punishment cell. One prisoner there was due for release in two days, so I asked him to get word about my situation to my family. A day later the guards transferred me to a solitary cell where I spent the next seven days alone.

The Lord was especially near to me in those trying days. I recalled Acts 21, how many people spoke against Paul's journey to Jersualem. Many people spoke against going there, warning of bonds and sorrows. But Paul answered, "What mean ye to weep and to break mine heart? for I am ready not to be bound only, but also to die at Jerusalem for the name of the Lord Jesus" (v. 13). Three years earlier in the Vladimir prison, I had searched my heart and asked whether I was ready to say the same as the apostle Paul. Was I ready not only to be in bonds, but even to die for the name of the Lord? At that time I had come to the conclusion that I was ready to be in bonds for the work of God but not to die for Christ. Now, during these seven days of isolation, the Lord somehow touched my heart in a special way. Thinking on Paul's words, I also was finally able to say, "I want to be ready to die for the name of the Lord Jesus."

So the Lord prepared my soul. But something unusual happened in my body: my heart started pounding so fiercely that it woke me up at night and would not let me sleep. In the afternoon this palpitation would begin again. Although I spent the next five months until the trial this way, after the trial my heart stopped bothering me; its normal rhythm was restored.

This time, like three years earlier, the most troubling thought was of postponing the wedding for an unknown length of time—maybe forever. I tried not to think about Nina and our hopes and plans; such thoughts were too painful. Of course, it was always comforting to know that Nina fully understood and supported me. When I proposed marriage to her, I had explained that my life was dedicated to the Lord and therefore many difficulties and trials could take place in our life together. I had asked her to consider seriously whether she was willing to share the fate of a minister—and possibly of a prisoner. Nina answered that she was ready for us to follow the Lord together, even if it meant traveling a path of bonds and suffering. Little did we know our sufferings would start even before our wedding!

For the trial I was driven to the prison in Krasnoyarsk and put on "death row." Since this cell had no mattress and the bed was made of iron, I did not sleep much at night. With my sack under my head, I lay right on the iron bed but would soon awaken because my side was freezing to the iron. I needed to turn over and over all night to keep from freezing. I was there for a month.

At the trial the authorities used two letters as charges against me. The first was the letter to my mother for which I had already sat in isolation for fifteen days. The second was a letter to Larisa Zaitseva from Rostov that they said contained "negative elements." (What these elements consisted of, I don't know to this day.) They also charged me with a photo album which I had filled with pictures received in letters from family and friends, with captions from letters, poems, or Bible verses. Supposedly it was slanderous in nature. At the time of the search, a *Herald of Truth* magazine was also taken away.

In the conclusion of scientific-ideological expertise it was stated, "The materials submitted for investigation contain knowingly false fabrications discrediting the Soviet government and social order. They are unswerving in their goal of fomenting ideological hostility in the reader in the way of discrimination of the policy of the Communisty Party of the Soviet Union and of the Soviet government in relation to religion, the church, and believers, inciting in their surroundings unhealthy sociopolitical displays, and in the final analysis to the creation of organized political opposition to the existence of the order in the USSR on the basis of the believing segment of our population. And likewise in the letters addressed by Kalyashin to Maria Kalyashina on May 25 of 1983, and in the photo album entitled 'My Wandering Years' is this idea of persecutions for faith similarly confirmed."

While examining the charges, I put in a request for the court to conduct another examination with the participation of lawyers who are experts in theological education—since my case delved into materials from the Christian magazine *Herald of Truth*, quotations from the Bible, and poems with Christian contents from my photo album, and I considered atheist experts incompetent in the appraisal of material of such a religious nature. After some time the investigator announced that my application for theological expertise had been refused, but that my case would be passed on to the prosecutor of the USSR for further examination.

Several days before the trial, the investigator brought me a defense attorney. I agreed to talk with her, but right away this woman said the conversation would be short because she was in a hurry.

"But this case will decide a man's life and several years in prison," I countered. "For me this is serious. I want to ask you legal questions that apply to me."

She hurriedly answered a question. However, when I began to write down what seemed important for my defense, she again interrupted, saying she was out of time and had to go.

"Larisa Georgievna," I said, "do you really not understand that I may be convicted, not for three weeks or for three months, but for three years or more? Your legal aid is vital, but you don't even want to take the time to understand my case and answer my questions. You must understand; everyone has his own fate, his own story, and you can't approach every case the same. I must refuse your defense at the trial."

My mother, Nina, and some friends managed to find out the day and place of the trial. Many young people from Krasnoyarsk Baptist Church also came. At first the authorities granted only a small room for the trial, so hardly anybody could come in. But after I asked the judge for a larger room, the next day this larger room was filled with Christian young people.

The *Herald of Truth* that had been confiscated from me received a lot of attention during the trial. "Why do you Baptists publish this magazine?" the judge asked.

"Would you publish articles with Christian contents in your newspapers and magazines?" I replied.

"Of course not! What a question!"

Then I explained how essential Christian literature is for believers and that *Herald of Truth* publishes articles on just such themes: spiritual edification, the lives and experiences of believers, and what is going on in churches across the country. "We love our magazine and need it," I added.

But the judge pressed on, "After all, Kalyashin, you know this magazine is forbidden! How in the world could you read it?"

"Our Christian magazine is precious to me," I responded. "I always read it."

The Lord amazingly blessed all the proceedings and disgraced the adversaries' intentions. God helped me to answer the questions in such a way that even the prosecutor got twisted around and didn't know what else to ask. Mama later told me that everyone in the courtroom felt I would be released, since the trial showed my innocence.

At one point I started to think about something and lowered my head in concentration. But Nina thought I had started to grieve, so she smiled at me and nodded, saying, "Heads up! Don't be sad!" I smiled back and again felt my heart warmed from her support.

The judge finally retired to the conference room, came back, and announced the sentence: two and a half years' deprivation of freedom. Friends began throwing flowers to me, but the guard rushed me out of the room.

After the trial I was put in a cell with forty other prisoners. Water dripped from the ceiling, so even the mattresses were damp. The prisoners did not greet me with much friendliness, but when I said I am a Christian, men who had been in camps with Veniamin Markevich, Oleg Popov, and Georgi Vins came over to talk to me.

"Do you know Georgi Vins?" one man asked.

"Yes, he's one of our ministers."

"When you see Vins, say hello from Kicel. We served time together in the Urals."

"I don't know if I'll see Georgi Vins again," I answered.

"He's no longer here. He's out of the country; his citizenship was taken away."

January 2 was my birthday. In the cell, of course, no one knew about it, and I didn't even want to mention it. Then after lunch a guard suddenly called me out.

"Are you transferring me to a different cell?" I asked. "Should I take my things with me?"

"No, don't take anything!"

I was led down to the visiting room! Nina and my little brother Eugene were already waiting for me! What a birthday surprise! We were granted a two-hour visit.

I spent eight months in the Krasnoyarsk prison. Every day we received soup made from salted cabbage, but it was sour and had a strange odor. I got the impression the pots were never washed, and each day's soup was cooked in the dirty pots from the day before. My stomach started aching. In the evening we got a watery wheat mush.

After eight months the guards called me out for transport and took me to a camp situated on the bank of the little river Beresa, in the middle of a beautiful forest. I simply rejoiced at the camp: fresh air, the sky overhead, the breeze. . . . One day later they had already assigned me to a job, but every evening after work I walked outside.

Soon Nina came to visit me, and we decided to submit an application for permission to hold a wedding ceremony right in the camp. (Of course, I was not going to object if she had decided to become the wife of a prisoner and to live apart for two years until the end of my term!) We turned in the application, and the authorities assigned June 10 for the registration of the wedding. Camp authorities tried to interfere with our wedding plans, but the Lord protected us and the wedding took place as scheduled. Our parents accompanied Nina; and the evangelist from the Dedovsk church, Nikolai Kruchinin, conducted the ceremony.

After the wedding, when my family and Nina had gone away, the authorities increasingly summoned me for discussions, threatening and intimidating me. Threatening to turn me over to the camp homosexuals, the prosecutor said, "I'll stick you in such a cell, and you know what they'll do to you there!"

"There's nothing worse than death you can do to me!" I answered.

He agreed. "Yes, that's true. There's nothing past death we can do to you."

"But death isn't frightening to me. I'm a Christian. If I die, I'll be in heaven with the Lord."

The prosecutor didn't answer; he just ordered me back to the barracks. That was the last of our discussions.

After several days I was unexpectedly summoned to the warden's office. I assumed that someone had come to interrogate me again, but it turned out quite differently. I was hurried onto a transport to another camp and not even permitted to gather my belongings to take along.

At the new camp they assigned me to the most backbreaking job: cutting timber. We worked twelve hours a day, and by the evening I was too exhausted even to step over a log. "Lord," I prayed, "if you allow an accident to happen to me, please help me not to complain and to receive everything with thankfulness to you."

The Lord heard my prayers, and after two weeks I was transferred to an easier job, where we worked only eight hours a day, leaving me spare time in the evenings to read and answer my letters. I remained in that camp for only three months; then I was sent on another transport. The escort guards told me I was being sent far away, all the way to the Ural Mountains. So this time I was sent westward from prison to prison: Krasnoyarsk, Omsk, Sverdlovsk, Perm, Kizel.

In the Sverdlovsk prison I met a prisoner called Joseph from the Ukraine. He told me he had known the Vins family in Kiev. He recalled Lydia Mikhailovna, the grandmother, with great respect and also told me Vins's daughter had given him a Bible, which had caused him and his wife to appreciate them all the more. "Yes," he said, "interesting people, you Baptists! I especially like how faithful your wives are to you, even when you're in prison and separated for many years. That's rare these days."

I spent only an hour and a half in the same cell with Joseph; then the guards put us in separate cells and we didn't see each other anymore. But our conversation stayed in my mind.

In the Kizel prison the guards put us in a basement cell where water covered the floor. The cell was large, so we had plenty of room. I had gotten tired on the train and immediately found myself a spot on the bunks and fell asleep. But through my sleep I heard a growing commotion. The prisoners who had been in the cell earlier began looking through and taking the belongings of the newcomers from my transport.

My turn came. Someone pushed me on the side and said, "Well, countryman, open your sack! Let's have a look at what you've got."

I raised my head. Before me stood an old Gypsy. (Later I learned he had served three terms of fifteen years each. Twice he had been sentenced to execution, but later the sentences were changed to fifteen years.)

"Here are my things. Have a look!" I said.

He began to pull everything out and saw that almost all my baggage consisted of letters. I then had more than a thousand letters.

"What's all this?" he asked.

"My mail!"

In wonder he asked, "Who writes to you?"

"My friends! I'm a Christian, so I have friends in every city, even around the whole world!"

"Give back his things!" he ordered the others. Later he told me he had met believers in other prisons and greatly respected them.

At last I arrived at my new camp. Right away the authorities there started creating special conditions for me. For example, they classified me as a difficult case even though I had not a single violation against me. And several prisoners told me that camp authorities were threatening them, demanding false reports that Kalyashin had forced conversations about God on them.

On May 7, 1986, I was called from work for an interrogation with two KGB workers in the warden's office. They had come from Perm and Kizel to question me about evangelist Vasily Yudintsev, who had just been arrested and charged with being the editor of *Herald of Truth*. I did not want to give any evidence against a minister and excused myself on the grounds that I had been a prisoner for five years and could hardly know what was happening in freedom. But then they threatened that I had better tell whether I knew Yudintsev personally and what his role in the church was while I was still free.

I refused to give any such information and told them bluntly that they had no right to pry into internal church matters. Infuriated, the KGB major from Perm began shouting. In the end he vowed to deprive me of a visit with my wife. That was exactly what I feared most, since

Nina was supposed to arrive for a visit the next day. I walked back to the barracks with a heavy heart. That very evening, however, I was astonished to be summoned for a meeting with Nina! How we rejoiced and thanked the Lord!

On the following day, when the operative officer came into the visiting room and saw me there, he was outraged: "Kalyashin, you're having a visit? Who authorized you to get a visit?"

"The camp warden signed the authorization," I told him.

He called for the warden and said the KGB men had told him to deprive me of a visit when he drove them to the train station the day before. But the warden had known nothing of these instructions, and Nina arrived a day early, while the operative officer had returned late at night. Since empty rooms were available, we had been granted a visit right away. By the Lord's mercy, Nina and I saw each other even though the KGB had decided otherwise!

For the five months prior to my release date I was repeatedly summoned by the KGB major from Kizel. First he wanted to know how I planned to live in freedom after my release. I answered that my life is dedicated to serve God and I would do anything in the church that the Lord assigns. Next he urged me to behave more carefully in freedom—and most importantly, not to hinder the KGB's work in the church.

Several days before the end of my term I received my checklist, but the camp authorities continued to exert great psychological pressure. I was worried. In prayer I asked the Lord, "Will I really be free in a few days—in the company of friends, at home with my wife? Or will it be like last time, getting transferred to prison on the day of my release?"

My last night in the camp I could not get to sleep. Morning dawned, and the prisoners went to work. By ten o'clock, I still had not been called to the guard house. At eleven-thirty I was finally summoned, and the guards did not even look through my things before I was led out the camp gates.

My loved ones were waiting outside! My little sister Nadia threw her arms around my neck. My wife's brother Pavel ran up; then everyone else gathered around. I was free! Five and a half years of bonds were behind me! But the desire of my heart was the same—to serve God faithfully. So right there at the gate, surrounded by family and friends, I thanked the Lord for all his grace on the path just trod.

I sincerely thank everyone who supported this captive Christian in prayer, in letters, or in petitions. Thank you for sharing my sufferings for Christ. As Jesus Christ said, "I was in prison, and ye came unto me." And the Lord, true to his promises, will repay you one hundredfold.

Aleksei was welcomed home by his wife Nina and their first child, born while Aleksei was still a prisoner.

Soon after his release Aleksei, in a solemn ceremony, was ordained to the ministry. Although he has been fined several times for holding prayer meetings in his home, he continues to preach and serve the Lord faithfully.

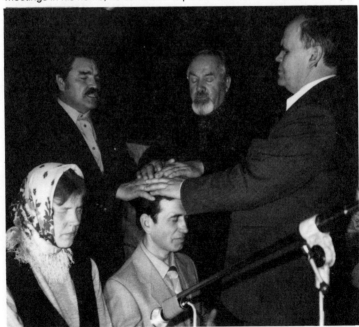

13

Nikolai Shepel
Ready to Suffer

Shortly before my first arrest (1963) I realized that great difficulties and trials lay ahead of me. Here's how it happened:

I had spent the evening with my elderly mother at her apartment, and as I walked back to the bus stop, I meditated on the Word of God and sang songs to myself. It was a long walk, and I was alone on the snowy streets. I was having a wonderful time of fellowship with the Lord when suddenly he put a question into my mind: "Do you love me?"

In January of 1984 Nikolai Shepel (b. 1938) was arrested in Tbilisi along with evangelist Peter Peters. Nikolai, then 45, was sentenced to three years' imprisonment, his second term. Released in 1987, he now lives with his wife, Ekaterina, in the village of Khutory. The Shepels have seven children.

With deep humility I responded, "Yes, Lord, you know I love you."

Then came a second question: "And are you ready to suffer for me?"

"Yes, Lord," I answered. "I'm ready."

Just then the bus screeched up and interrupted my thoughts. A few days later, while at work, I was called into the supervisor's office. The police were already waiting with a warrant for my arrest.

From the moment I stepped into the prison cell I had opportunities to witness for Christ. The other prisoners immediately surrounded me and started asking, "Who are you? What are you in prison for?" I told them I was a Christian and had been arrested for preaching the gospel.

I ended up getting along very well with the other prisoners, but it was a little rough at first. From my very first day in that cell I made it a rule that as soon as the evening bell rang and the other prisoners lay down to sleep, I would kneel beside my bunk to pray. But several of my cellmates tried to disturb me. As I prayed the first night, someone balanced a book on my head. They all waited to see how I would react, but I ignored the book and continued praying. When I finished I took the book off my head, put it on the table, and lay down to sleep. For the next night they came up with another idea. They had worked all day to make a small cross. While I prayed, they laid it across my arms. Again I did not react. At the end of my prayers I just set the cross on the table and went to bed. The third night they dropped a blanket over my head. I went on praying, and when I finished I removed the blanket and lay down to sleep.

It was not until twenty years later that I saw the fruit of my Christian testimony in that investigation cell. One night at home I heard a knock on the window. "Who's there?" I called.

"Nikolai, open up!" I heard someone say. Although I failed to recognize the voice, I opened the door and there stood Viktor, a man who, twenty years earlier, had been in that cell with me!

"I have to talk to you," he said, so I invited him to come in and sit down.

"My life is a wreck," he began, "and today I finally decided to do something about it. I decided to take my car out, get it going as fast as I could, and smash it into a tree. Then suddenly I thought of you. I remembered how you prayed in that cell. So I decided to come see you first, and then whatever happens, happens."

Viktor and I talked until morning, and when he left I gave him a Gospel. Not long afterward he and his wife both turned to Christ and joined the church. The ways of the Lord are simply amazing!

After my first arrest and many days in the investigation cell, I had finally been tried. Three of us believers were sentenced together: another preacher, a young Christian lady, and me. My sentence was the worst—three years in a prison, followed by two years in a labor camp under strict regime, and five years of exile, plus the confiscation of my property.

As the other brother and I were being transported to the prison in Kharkov, I learned that we were considered especially dangerous criminals. The guards separated us from the rest of the prisoners on the train and watched us in a special car.

By the time I arrived in Kharkov, I thought that I was already fairly familiar with prison because I had been in the investigation cell for such a long time. But when I saw this place—the concrete, iron, and gloom—I said, "Oh Lord, is it possible to survive in such a place?" But, after being there for a year and a half, I thanked God for the great lesson He taught me, that truly it is possible to live anywhere as long as God is with you.

I had already learned that one of the most wearing things about prison is the glaring lights. They are kept on twenty-four hours a day, endlessly irritating the eyes. But the work in the Kharkov prison added another kind of pain. We worked with chemicals and had to handle caustic materials that burned our hands and arms. It was torturous work, and there was no way to get out of it. But the Lord freed me of it in answer to the prayers of the church.

The warden needed a draftsman and started asking around for one among the prisoners. When someone told him that I knew drafting, he called me in for a talk. He assigned me to work in the office, and it was such a wonderful change. I made blueprints at a desk in a clean room, and sometimes during working hours I was allowed to go outside and breathe fresh air. In a closed prison, fresh air is valued more highly than food. This was such a special blessing from God! But an even greater blessing came after eighteen months of prison life. I was rehabilitated, so I ended up serving only part of my term! This was not, however, my last conflict with the authorities.

By 1984 our church was under increasing pressure from the authorities to register. But since the conditions of registration were unacceptable, we voted to reject registration unanimously. Then the authorities began putting special pressure on me personally as a pastor of the church. For example, a meeting was held in my department at work, and several people who had been coached by the authorities got up and made slanderous speeches against Christians. Their comments were so groundless that it was frustrating even to sit still and listen. Finally I was offered seven minutes to reply. I started to explain the situation to my co-workers, but you cannot say much in just seven minutes.

When my time ran out, several men said, "Let him keep talking. Give him another seven minutes." When the next seven minutes were up, my co-workers again demanded I be allowed to continue without interruption. My time was extended again, and I was able to explain fully why, as a Christian, I could never meet government demands that contradicted the Word of God. Everyone listened closely. After I finished, though, the agent from the Department of Religious Cults stood up and made atrocious, false accusations against believers. Then the group voted. Everyone who agreed that I had broken the law was told to raise his hand. But the voting was conducted illegally. No one ever counted how many people disagreed or abstained from voting. After the meeting many of the workers shook my hand and said, "Stick with what you believe. Don't let anyone change your mind."

After that meeting I was sure I would be arrested again. My wife and I talked it over. She was a tremendous encouragement. She supported me completely, saying she was ready for anything. I had complete personal peace and trusted the Lord, but it was reassuring to know that my family stood with me.

The Lord let me work in freedom a little longer. Then, on the way home from a pastors' meeting, I was arrested at a train station. I was driven to the prison in Cherkassy, and all the way there I talked to the policemen about Jesus Christ. They didn't even put handcuffs on me!

While in prison during the investigation, I found out that two other ministers from my church—evangelist Aleksandr Pavlenko and music director Anatoly Ivaschenko—had been arrested after me and that we were to be tried together. This was painful news. It meant the church was left without ministers. I never saw my two friends inside the prison, but we were driven to the trial in the same car and were able to pray together.

The trial was held at the factory where I had worked. Many workers and fellow Christians attended. In the "courtroom" we three bore witness to God and stood firm to our Christian convictions. In the end I was sentenced to three years' imprisonment, and the other two ministers received two and a half years each.

As soon as the verdict was read, our friends threw us flowers and shouted, "Take courage! We're praying for you!" The guards grabbed the flowers away, but we were greatly encouraged by this demonstration of love. During the drive back to prison, we prayed together one last time and then said good-bye. The guards separated us at the prison, just as we expected.

I was sent to a camp in Cherkassy, not far from home. Several other Christians served terms at that camp, so as soon as the other prisoners found out I am a believer, they said, "Oh, we know your people! They're good people—dependable, friendly. They always tell the truth and help each other." It was a special blessing to hear such testimony about Christians on my first day in camp. These words were also a good lesson that we should always live in such a way that the light of Christ can be seen by all. Later I met two other Christians in the camp, and we had a joyous meeting.

As I look back, I divide my term of imprisonment in Cherkassy into three periods. The first was a period of fervent prayer that God would use our testimonies in the camp, that he would grant a spiritual awakening among the prisoners, and that our years in bonds would not be wasted. When we met for fellowship, we always reminded each other that God had not brought us there just to serve our sentences, but to work for him and win souls for his kingdom. So first we prayed for God's blessing. Second came a period of answers to our prayers, and we saw much fruit. Third, there followed a period of fiery trials, but even then we saw special blessings from the Lord.

The first period lasted for about a year. I was working as an on-call electrician. I worked alone in a small room and was called out only when something needed fixing right away. Sometimes I had night duty, and I spent the quiet hours praying and reading a little Gospel I had. After that year I was transferred to another job where I was constantly surrounded by people, but this change gave me opportunities for many good conversations about the Lord.

The other two Christians and I decided that even though there were only a few of us, we would consider ourselves the camp church. We each took on a ministry according to our gifts and abilities. For instance, one brother was responsible for looking after material needs. All three of us shared the food parcels we received so that no one would suffer need. In this ministry we also included the prisoners who were beginning to take an interest in the things of the Lord. A second brother was responsible for evangelism, because the Lord had given him this gift. He could strike up a conversation with anyone at any time. I was given the responsibility of discipling the prisoners who came to the Lord and

Nikolai's family reads a letter they received from him during his imprisonment.

wanted to know more about the Word of God and the principles of the Christian life.

I rejoiced to see God's leading in my life because, while I served the church in freedom, God had trained me for just such a prison ministry. One of the new Christians, Vasily, waited for me every day after work and would always say, "Let's talk for a while." Later I noticed that he was sharing his faith with others. It was such a joy to see a new Christian begin to labor for the Lord.

Of course, all the new believers faced great trials and pressures from the camp authorities. One of them, Kolya, went through such testing after his conversion that he ended up in the prison hospital. To this day I don't know what happened to him or where he is.

We decided not to baptize any of the new Christians in the camp. Instead we gave them the names and addresses of believers in their home towns and recommended that they be baptized by the local churches.

During the third period of my imprisonment, the KGB started coming to the camp to talk to me. They offered me a lot of privileges and even early release if I agreed to become their informant. When I refused, the camp authorities began harassing me. They accused me falsely of breaking camp rules. One time there was something "wrong" with my uniform; the next time they felt that my haircut did not conform to regulations. Then on December 27 my wife and seven children traveled to the camp to see me. They registered at the office, and the visit was approved, but then the guards came to my barracks to search my things and "found" twenty-five rubles in my pillowcase.

"Look!" said the officer. "Shepel is hiding money!"

I was taken straight to the warden's office and sentenced to seven days in a punishment cell.

"But I have a visit scheduled, and my wife and children are here already," I protested.

"Well, we'll just have to tell your wife not to sneak money to you anymore," the warden answered. Of course, this was a complete mockery because everyone knew the money had been planted in my pillowcase.

"But I'm sick," I said. "I'm being treated for an acute ulcer. How can you put me in the punishment cell?"

The warden called for the head of the infirmary to bring my medical file. "Can Shepel be put in the punishment cell in his condition?"

The doctor said yes, so I was taken to the punishment cell. This was really an ordeal for me. It is hard to express how badly I wanted to see my family! I spent almost the entire seven days in fasting. But even in solitary confinement the Lord sent me an unexpected blessing. Another prisoner was in my cell. As we started talking, he told me about his life. In turn, I was able to talk with him about Christ and salvation. Then, on New Year's Eve, the man asked me, "How does a person become a Christian? What should I do to be saved?" We prayed together, and he asked God to forgive his sins. Talk about joy! Later this man admitted to me that he had planned to commit suicide that very night. He pulled out a ten-foot rope that he had hidden in the cot. I was amazed that the guards had not found it—they searched everything so carefully. Satan had done all he could to insure that another soul would be in his power forever. But God overruled and gave this man salvation and eternal life.

After being in the punishment cell, I got very sick and was put in the prison hospital for a time. But for the next eight months I suffered serious heart problems. My heart just didn't want to work right, and I was positive I would not live long enough to see my family and friends again. I managed to send a note to my wife with a Bible verse that said, ". . . deliver them that are drawn into death . . ." (Prov. 24:11).

A few months before my term ended, my living conditions improved noticeably. First I started getting good medical treatment. Then the warden summoned me to his office. "Write to your wife," he said, "and tell her that things are better for you now. Tell her they don't need to write any more petitions. Otherwise we have to spend all our time answering the letters we get about you."

This made me realize just how important it is to pray and petition on behalf of God's prisoners. It is a tremendous ministry of compassion and support. I was greatly encouraged to learn that so many friends had responded to my cry for help. Praise God!

I had one other weight hanging over me the whole time I was in the camp. The court had decided to deprive my wife and myself of our parental rights and take away our younger children because we were teaching them about God. My greatest comfort during this time was the knowledge that God holds everything in his hands and that he will never allow us to be tested beyond our strength. I also knew how firm and unwavering my wife is in following the Lord, and this, too, reassured me.

During those years I often thought of Psalm 71:5: "For thou art my hope, O Lord God: thou art my trust from my youth." I knew that everyone who constantly trusts God in everything will never be ashamed.

The day of my release was drawing near. In camp you always start saying good-bye to everyone well in advance. I had my final talks with the new believers. They rejoiced with me that soon I would be home with my family, but some said, "We still need you here. It's terrible even to say it, but we wish you could stay a little longer."

On my last day I went to the camp office to get my documents. The warden was there. Despite all the evil he had done to me during my time in camp, I said, "Thank you, Warden, for everything."

"What?" he replied, astonished. "What are you thanking me for?"

"For everything," I answered, and of course he knew what I meant. I knew that if he had any conscience left, he would think about it. Then I stepped back into the snowstorm outside.

Just before I was supposed to leave the camp, however, I was suddenly called back to the office. "You've been here three years," the warden said, "and you haven't shown any sign of rehabilitation. Therefore you'll be on probation for a year." Generally a person is informed of probation well before he is released, but I was told about it just ten minutes before walking out the gate.

"Thank you for the probation," I said to the warden.

At a crowded house church service, Nikolai gives praise to God for his faithfulness and mercy.

In the spring of 1988, Nikolai Shepel was a featured speaker at a Christian youth rally near Kiev.

My response made him very uncomfortable. "What do you mean?" he asked. "Do you think it was my idea?" When he said this, I realized that he was simply carrying out someone else's orders. I went back out into the cold.

Because of the tremendous snowstorm that day, my friends could not get to the camp to meet me, and I had a hard time getting a ride to the train station. But there, at last, I saw my wife and friends who were on their way to the camp. They took me home, where the children had strung up a banner that said, "Welcome home, dearest Papa!" Many friends came to the house to greet me, so before I even had a chance to change out of my prison uniform, we had a worship service right then to thank God.

Now, looking back over my life, I can say that God has revealed his mercy and love in many ways—even in the middle of the worst circumstances. Every Christian faces trials, but when the righteous man remains true to the Lord, then God sends blessings. The main thing to remember is this: when a Christian is faithful, God is glorified. He will use our trials and hard experiences to make his name known.

A Soviet prison camp.

Opposite:
Soviet police outside a
worship service.

Police breaking up a house
church service.

Friends wait outside the
entrance to a courtroom
where a brother in Christ
is on trial.

Prisoners at Omsk, Siberia.
Mikhail Khorev endured the
tortures of the *Afrikanka*
punishment cell here.

A Christian prisoner behind bars.

Children have a visible and active part in worship services. This assures that faith in Jesus Christ will be handed down from generation to generation, something which irritates atheistic authorities.

Biographical Supplement

Artiushenko, Boris. Born 1920, died 1984. Home town was Kursk. Pastor Artiushenko completed three terms in bonds. Four months after his fourth arrest for preaching, he died on an operating table in a prison hospital. The official diagnosis was a perforated ulcer of the duodenum.

Balatsky, Anatoly. Born 1939. Wife's name is Galina. Home town is Voroshilovgrad. Has served three terms.

Baturin, Nikolai. Born 1927, died 1988. Wife's name is Valentina. Seven children. Home town is Shakhty. Pastor Baturin served six terms in bonds for his ministry of preaching and serving as secretary of the Council of Evangelical Baptist Churches. When he learned that a seventh case was being opened against him, he went into hiding and served the CEBC from underground. He died of a heart attack while alone at home.

Biblenko, Ivan. Born 1928, died 1975. Wife's name is Taisa. Home town was Krivoi Rog. Served one term.

Boiko, Nikolai. Born 1922. Wife's name is Valentina. Seven children (originally eight, but one died). Formerly ministering in Odessa, Pastor Boiko currently lives in exile in the village of Ayan in Khabarovsk krai. His treatment in labor camp was particularly abusive. At the beginning of his present term (his third) authorities said, "You won't believe in God here. We'll break you. And if we don't break you, we'll let you rot!" As a result of their efforts, he

261

spent months in punishment cells. He suffers from heart damage and partial paralysis.

Bublik, Sergei. Born 1957. Wife's name is Ludmila. Home town is Rostov-na-Donu. Has served a three-year term for printing Bibles.

Bystrova, Tamara. Born 1949. She is single, and her mother has died. Home town is Narva. This woman has served a three-year term for printing Bibles.

Chistyakov, Veniamin. Born 1935. Wife's name is Lubov. Eleven children. Home town is Ordzhonikidze. Has served one term.

Didnyak, Maria. Born 1933. Husband's name is Vasily (he is not a Christian). Two children. Home town is Nikolaev. Has served one term.

Goryanin, Mikhail. Born 1951. Wife's name is Vera. Home town is Tikhoretsk. Six children. Has served one term.

Ivaschenko, Anatoly. Born 1952. Wife's name is Nadezhda. Four children. Home town is Cherkassy. This man is the son of exiled pastor Yakov Ivaschenko. He has served one term for being a youth leader and music director in his church.

Khmara, Nikolai. Born 1916, died 1964. Wife's name is Maria. Four children. Home town was Kulunda. Nikolai Khmara became a Christian and was baptized with his wife in July 1963. He opened his house for worship services and was arrested on November 5. On trial from December 24 to 27, he was sentenced to three years. On January 11, 1964, Maria received a telegram to come for her dead husband's body. The body was covered with bruises, with burn marks on the hands and feet. The stomach had been punctured, and his tongue was gone.

Klassen, Rudolph. Born 1931. Wife's name is Talita. Home town is Karaganda, where Pastor Klassen ministers. Has served three terms. After his last release, he told his church, "As Christians it is our privilege to suffer reproaches and tribulation not only for our own testimony, but also for standing by others who are persecuted for Christ's sake."

Kruchinin, Nikolai. Born 1943. Wife's name is Ludmila. Seven children. Home town is Dedovsk, a suburb of Moscow. Has served two terms.

Krugovikh, Aleksandr. Born 1946. Wife's name is Tamara. Five children. Home town is Makeyevka. Has served one term.

Kryuchkov, Gennady. Born 1926. The president of CEBC. Wife's name is Lydia. Nine children. The Kryuchkov family lives in the city of Tula, where their home is under surveillance. Since 1970 Pastor Kryuchkov has been compelled to live and conduct his underground ministry away from his family and in hiding from the KGB. He served one term in bonds from 1966 to 1969.

Mikhin, Vasily. Born 1933. Wife's name is Tatyana. Nine children. Home town is Ordzhonikidze. Has served one term.

Minyakov, Dmitri. Born 1921. Five children. Dmitri's first wife, Antonina, died in 1980 while he was conducting his Christian ministry in hiding. His second wife's name is Ksenya. Dmitri has served three terms for preaching and being a leader of the CEBC. Before his last arrest in 1981, he wrote, "We will stand in truth as long as God gives us life. Our only desire is to remain faithful to Him." Today his health is shattered, and little strength is left in his body as his wife nurses him. But he remains faithful to God.

Moiseyev, Ivan ("Vanya"). Born 1952, died 1972. Conscripted into the Soviet Army (military unit 71-96-8), Vanya was repeatedly threatened, harassed, and punished for his Christian convictions. At age 20 he was brutally tortured and drowned by the military in the Azov Sea near the city of Kerchi. The story of his faithfulness to Christ has been retold and published around the world.

Mosha, Viktor. Born 1935. Wife's name is Nina. Home town is Dergachi. Viktor is an energetic minister whose fast-paced vibrant sermons make him a favorite among children and young people. For his ministry he has served four terms in bonds.

Nikitkov, Aleksander. Born 1934. Wife's name is Zinaida. Six children. Home town is Ryazan. Has served two terms, suffering a heart attack at the Ryazan prison during the second term.

Odintsov, Nikolai. Born 1870, died 1939(?). Wife's name was Alexandra. Lived outside Moscow. Nikolai Odintsov was the president of the Federated Union of Baptists in the Soviet Union. In 1928 he headed the Baptist delegation from the Soviet Union to the Fourth World Baptist Congress in Toronto, Canada. However, Soviet authorities arrested him shortly afterward for his ministry. His wife gained one last visit with him in 1937 in Siberia. After World War II, other Christians testified that he had died during a transport between prison camps, eaten alive by guard dogs.

Pavlenko, Alexander. Born 1952. Wife's name is Nadezhda. Four children. Home town is Cherkassy. Has served one term.

Popov, Nikolai. Born 1927. Wife's name is Nadezhda. Eight children. Home town is Ryazan. Has served three terms.

Popov, Oleg. Born 1954. Wife's name is Tatyana. Four children. Home town is Ryazan. Has served one term. Oleg is the son of Nikolai Popov and spent time imprisoned in the same tower where his father was once held.

Rytikov, Pavel. Born 1930. Wife's name Galina. Ten children. Home town is Krasnodon. Pastor Rytikov has served four terms for preaching, ministering with the CEBC, and teaching Christianity to children. From bonds he wrote, "Do not get carried away by the pleasures of this world, for the friendship of the world is enmity with God. Don't be captive of the thinking and aims of the world that surround you, but obey God and live as Christ taught us."

Sazhnev, Pavel. Born 1952. Wife's name is Vera. Five children. Home town is Voroshilovgrad. Has served one term.

Shokha, Pyotr. Born 1909. Wife's name is Iosifa. Ten children. Home town is Saki. Has served three terms in bonds. At age 79, Pastor Shokha was arrested at a worship service and indicted for assaulting a local policeman. At the trial the strong, young "victim" looked embarrassed at the obviously fabricated charges. Nevertheless, the judge pronounced Pastor Shokha guilty.

Skornyakov, Yakov. Born 1928. Wife's name is Nina. Nine children. Home town is Dzhambul. Pastor Skornyakov has served three terms in bonds for pastoring and working with the CEBC. In a letter from camp he wrote, "We are strong even in death, so that we are able to pray for our tormentors and executioners." When he was released from camp after his last two combined terms (eight years), he was able to bring back the 9,546 letters he received from Christians in freedom.

Timchuk, Vladimir. Born 1959. Wife's name is Ludmila. Home town is Moscow. Has served one term.

Tyagun, Ivan. Born 1930. Wife's name is Elena. Seven children. Home town is Kirovsk. Has served one term.

Vilchinskaya, Galina. Born 1958. Galina's family (Zinaida and Vladimir) lives in Brest, but she has married Ivan Shapoval and now lives in Novokuznetsk. She has served two terms for teaching the Bible to children at a summer camp.

Vins, Lydia Mikhailovna. Born 1907, died 1985. Wife of American missionary Peter Vins and mother of Georgi Vins. Served one term at age 63 for working as director of the Council of Prisoners' Relatives. She joined her son in exile in America, where she continued to labor for Russian Christians until her death.

Vlasenko, Vladimir. Born 1954. Wife's name is Ludmila. Two children. Home town is Nikolaev. Has served one term.

Yudintsev, Serafima. Born 1938. Husband's name is Vasily. Thirteen children. Home town is Khartsyzsk. This woman was sentenced to a two-year term, to begin when her youngest child turned five years old, but the court later dropped the sentence.

Yudintsev, Vasily. Born 1931. Wife's name is Serafima. Thirteen children. Home town Khartsyzsk. Has served two terms for pastoring and ministering with the CEBC. He was held in prison and interrogated for thirteen days before authorities would confirm that he had been arrested.

Zaitseva, Larisa. Born 1951. Mother's name is Anastasia. Home town is Rostov-na-Donu. Has served two terms for work on Bible printing teams.

Zinchenko, Pavel. Born 1952. Wife's name is Tatyana. Four children. Home town is Kharkov. Has served one term.

Glossary

Articles of the Criminal Codes:

Article 70 (of the RSFSR Criminal Code): Anti-Soviet agitation and propaganda.

Article 128 (of the Ukrainian Criminal Code): Violation of the laws on the separation of church and state and of school and church.

Article 187–1 (of the Ukrainian Criminal Code): Circulation of deliberately false concoctions, slandering the Soviet state and social order.

Article 187–3 (of the Ukrainian Criminal Code): Organization of, or active participation in, group actions which disrupt public order.

Article 190–1 (of the RSFSR Criminal Code): Circulation of deliberately false concoctions, slandering the Soviet state and social order.

Article 190–3 (of the RSFSR Criminal Code): Organization of, or active participation in, group actions which disrupt public order.

Article 227 (of the RSFSR Criminal Code): Infringement of the person and rights of citizens under the guise of performing religious rituals.

AUCECB—All-Union Council of Evangelical Christians-Baptists. The group of registered churches whose leaders compromised biblical principles in order to win favor and recognition from the Soviet government. Also known as "registered Baptists."

"black raven." Nickname given to the type of vehicle used to transport prisoners short distances.

CEBC—Council of Evangelical Baptist Churches. The elected leadership of the persecuted Evangelical Baptist Churches, which refuse to compromise biblical principles in order to gain government sanction. Their churches are not registered with the government and meet in private houses, apartments, or forests. Also known as "unregistered Baptists."

CPR—Council of Prisoners' Relatives. The organization of women who have husbands or other family members in bonds for their Christian faith. This council gathers information on Christian prisoners and coordinates aid for their families.

investigation cell. A special prison cell where the Soviet authorities hold citizens suspected of illegal activities while a government prosecutor questions them and prepares materials for the case against them. Time spent in an investigation cell ranges from days to months and is counted as part of the prisoner's eventual sentence.

krai. A huge territorial division found in the Russian republic; larger than an oblast.

oblast. A territorial division within a Soviet republic, similar to a county.

operative division. The agency that performs the work of the KGB inside a Soviet prison or prison camp.

taiga. Swampy coniferous Siberian forest beginning where the tundra ends.

troinik cell. A small cell meant to hold three prisoners.

To learn more about the lives of Evangelical Baptists in the Soviet Union, write:
Georgi P. Vins
International Representation, Inc.
P. O. Box 1188
Elkhart, Indiana 46515
U.S.A.